# POINTS OF *View*

## Landscape Quilts to Stitch and Embellish

Valerie Hearder

*Martingale*®
& COMPANY

## CREDITS

President & CEO ~ Tom Wierzbicki
Publisher ~ Jane Hamada
Editorial Director ~ Mary V. Green
Managing Editor ~ Tina Cook
Developmental Editor ~ Karen Costello Soltys
Technical Editor ~ Ellen Pahl
Copy Editor ~ Melissa Bryan
Design Director ~ Stan Green
Assistant Design Director ~ Regina Girard
Illustrators ~ Laurel Strand & Adrienne Smitke
Cover & Text Designer ~ Shelly Garrison
Photographer ~ Brent Kane

Points of View: Landscape Quilts to Stitch and Embellish
© 2007 by Valerie Hearder

That Patchwork Place® is an imprint of Martingale & Company®.

Martingale & Company
20205 144th Ave. NE
Woodinville, WA 98072-8478
www.martingale-pub.com

Printed in China
12 11 10 09 08 07     8 7 6 5 4 3 2 1

**Library of Congress Cataloging-in-Publication Data**
Library of Congress Control Number: 2007018485

ISBN: 978-1-56477-700-3

Sulky is a registered trademark of Sulky of America.

## MISSION STATEMENT
Dedicated to providing quality products
and service to inspire creativity.

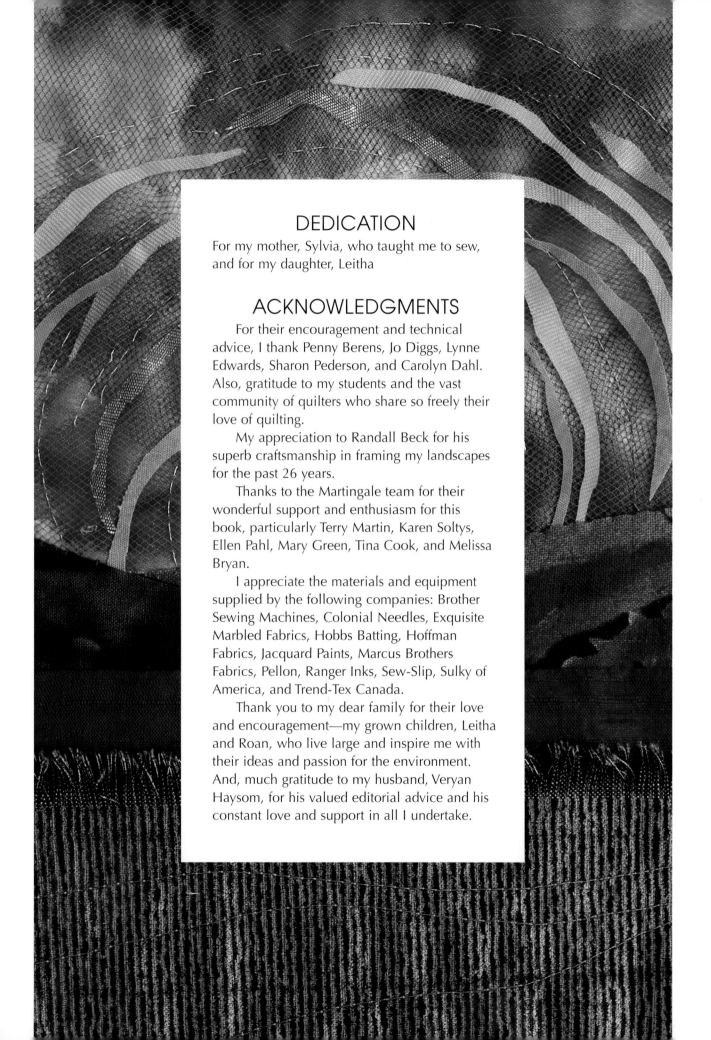

## DEDICATION

For my mother, Sylvia, who taught me to sew, and for my daughter, Leitha

## ACKNOWLEDGMENTS

For their encouragement and technical advice, I thank Penny Berens, Jo Diggs, Lynne Edwards, Sharon Pederson, and Carolyn Dahl. Also, gratitude to my students and the vast community of quilters who share so freely their love of quilting.

My appreciation to Randall Beck for his superb craftsmanship in framing my landscapes for the past 26 years.

Thanks to the Martingale team for their wonderful support and enthusiasm for this book, particularly Terry Martin, Karen Soltys, Ellen Pahl, Mary Green, Tina Cook, and Melissa Bryan.

I appreciate the materials and equipment supplied by the following companies: Brother Sewing Machines, Colonial Needles, Exquisite Marbled Fabrics, Hobbs Batting, Hoffman Fabrics, Jacquard Paints, Marcus Brothers Fabrics, Pellon, Ranger Inks, Sew-Slip, Sulky of America, and Trend-Tex Canada.

Thank you to my dear family for their love and encouragement—my grown children, Leitha and Roan, who live large and inspire me with their ideas and passion for the environment. And, much gratitude to my husband, Veryan Haysom, for his valued editorial advice and his constant love and support in all I undertake.

# CONTENTS

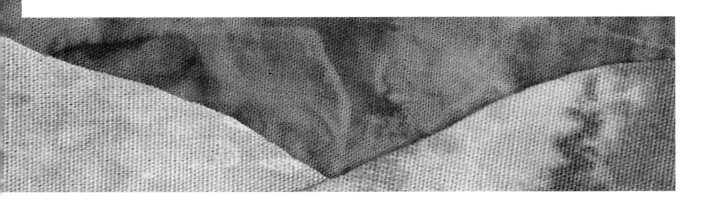

*Lifeline: Displacement by Valerie Hearder, 60" x 40".*
*From the collection of Lynne Edwards.*

"**We all have a home** landscape, a place from our childhood whose light, space and scale are the benchmark for all other landscapes we see. We carry our home landscape around with us. So it's not necessary to live in this landscape to be influenced by it."

—John Hartman, Canadian painter

My love of fabric was fostered in the vibrant, jostling, steaming-hot marketplaces of South Africa. I was born in Durban on the Indian Ocean and, as a teenager, I loved to search out exotic Indian silk saris, sarongs from Swaziland, and African indigo prints. The fabrics were cheap and irresistible. I didn't make anything with them; I just collected them. Then, at 20, my lifelong passion for quilting was sparked by a book on English patchwork paper piecing given to me by my mother. At 24 I left the Tropics to join my husband in Canada's Arctic. I arrived with two bags, one of which was filled with my beloved African fabrics that gave me much solace as I slowly adjusted to the frozen world of the North.

I taught myself how to make framed miniature fabric landscapes when we settled in Nova Scotia in 1981. I have often thought about their genesis and what they represent to me. The powerful landscapes of Africa and the magnificent northlands of Canada have had a big impact on my life. These environments have influenced and enriched my work for almost 30 years. They have become part of the tissue of my being, influencing the colors and forms that I have an affinity for and that emerge in my work. However, my small landscapes are largely impressionistic, imaginary responses to the fabric at hand, not faithful renditions of specific places, and so I begin part 1 by discussing fabric and how I select and use it in my work.

Reading the section "Fabric: Our Paint Palette" before you start the projects is important, as fabric is the cornerstone of my approach to making landscapes. If you can't find exactly the same fabric that I've used, and most likely you won't, that's not a problem—it's a design opportunity! The projects in this book are all based on the inspiration of fabric. The first project is "The Basic Landscape" (page 15), which provides all the keys to my pattern method and introduces you to the process for making my landscapes. Subsequent projects are featured in part 2, beginning on page 38. Each of these includes one or more additional techniques and design suggestions to create elegant results. With each new project and at each step of the way, you'll acquire skills and ideas that you can use for your own landscape designs. Once you have made the "Basic Landscape," you can dive into any project that catches your fancy. If you dive into making a project in part 2 first, please be prepared to refer back to part 1 for the pattern key and details of various techniques. With that said, I believe if you are willing to dive, you know how to swim—so go for it!

My approach is to use easy techniques and readily obtainable, nontoxic materials. The small size of the projects encourages experimentation and there is delight and satisfaction in making a beautiful project that is completed quickly. While my goal is to offer you projects that will stand as pieces you will be proud of, my intention is that you will use these projects as a starting point to explore design and technique and to add your own touch through fabrics, beads, and stitches.

Some landscapes are framed in a mat and others are quilted wall hangings, but all of them have simple elements that focus on the use of color, fabric, and embellishment techniques. Their small scale invites careful examination of fabric as one is drawn in to search for visual textures, colors, and patterns to use for the landscape elements. The process of choosing fabrics and composing the landscape is an enriching design exercise. Each project includes Design Ideas and Technique Tips to encourage you to try out different options and make changes to the patterns.

For me, making landscapes is a journey—one that has literally taken me around the world, as I have the good fortune to travel and teach landscape design in many countries. My hope is that this book will be a creative journey for you as well—one that will take you on byways of experimentation and discovery—and that you, too, will enjoy the delights of making landscapes. With this in mind, the guidelines in part 3, "Beyond Patterns," are intended to encourage you to develop your own sense of direction, travel beyond patterns, and create your own unique landscapes. The Gallery has beautiful landscapes from guest artists who will inspire you with their unique approaches. I'd love to see the landscapes you make from these projects and those of your own design! You're welcome to contact me through my Web site, listed under Resources at the end of the book.

Valerie
Mahone Bay, Nova Scotia, Canada

# FABRIC: OUR PAINT PALETTE

A love of fabric drives our passion for quilting. Fabric is also the "paint" for textile landscapes, and it provides the richest source of inspiration. When I start working on a landscape, I don't rely on photographs for inspiration; I turn to my fabrics to generate the designs. After teaching myself to make quilts in the English paper-piecing style using fabrics I had collected in the African markets, I made my first miniature, framed landscapes 26 years ago using fabrics that were commercially available at that time—mostly small calico prints. These gave the landscapes a naive, folksy feel. Today the market is bursting with rich batiks, hand-dyes, and designer prints from around the globe, all of which provide abundant inspiration for making landscapes. And, yes, you can still find those calicoes, perhaps at the back of your stash drawer, and go for a folk-art look, if that's your fancy.

## SEEING FABRIC WITH FRESH EYES

Looking at fabrics is the first creative step to making landscapes. Perhaps your initial instincts are that you have no landscape-type fabrics in your stash. But don't make your rush to judgment a rush to go fabric shopping—at least, not just yet! Pick any project in this book, focus on a single landform segment, and you'll notice it's the textural pattern in the fabric that turns the simple shape into something interesting in the context of the landscape. Then, take a long, loving look through your stash in the same way. One of the richest skills you can develop is being able to see the design potential beyond the obvious. A landscape composition becomes memorable when you add a piece of fabric filled with personal history and associations—plus a dash of the unexpected.

Something quite wonderful happens when you zero in on small areas of fabric as you search for landform elements. Your eye evaluates the fabric for how it may be able to communicate a lake or sandy beach. You're drawn into fine details as you imagine different ways to collage the details into a landscape based on your own interpretation of the print. The process is different from how we tend to look at fabric when making a geometric quilt. I've noticed, from years of teaching, that many people leave my landscape workshops seeing fabrics in a new way. It's like flexing a new muscle. The eye learns to discern different aspects of the fabric by seeking out patterns, designs, textures, and colors with a free-form collage landscape in mind. And there's a bonus: this new way of seeing informs your fabric choices for other quilt projects.

Viewfinders and frames are an integral part of my design methods. A viewfinder is such a simple tool, yet has a powerful way of helping the eye focus. Make a paper viewfinder by cutting two L shapes, 2" wide, from an 8½" x 11" piece of paper. Form the shapes into an adjustable window that you can slide across your fabric, making the opening bigger or smaller as needed to help you isolate just the right part to use as a landscape element.

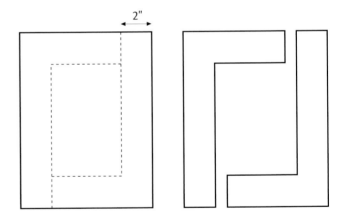

I also use tracing-paper templates to help in selecting fabrics or parts of fabrics (see "Template Pattern" on page 13). The template pattern is laid on the fabric to mark the cutting line and, since the print is discernible through the tracing paper, you can see what part of the fabric you want to cut. This is the moment when you make a personal choice about color, pattern, and form that will, piece by landform piece, make the finished landscape uniquely yours.

## ESTABLISHING YOUR LANDSCAPE FABRIC COLLECTION

The majority of the fabrics used in my projects are commercially printed. Examine the project photos, as well as the fabric swatches shown in this section, to get an idea of how I use and interpret fabric. You'll notice that I don't necessarily use obvious landscape fabrics and I seldom use fabric printed with ready-made landscape elements. I relish the search for unusual and unpredictable choices—like finding a mountain range in a fish print, or a river valley in a flowery petal fabric. The delight and creativity of using commercial "found" fabric lies in using it to convey a totally different meaning: the more unexpected the fabric, the more satisfaction I get from working it into a landscape.

When I'm buying fabric, my main priority is to look for interesting patterns in the print. When I find something intriguing, I audition it for its landscape potential by folding it to isolate the parts of the pattern that might be useful.

I seldom use all the same type of fabric in a landscape—say, all hand-dyes or all batiks. I find the landscapes, and also quilts for that matter, have more vitality when different fabrics are mixed together in a design.

I also don't limit my landscapes to classic, obvious nature colors. I like vibrant, rich color and have found that unusual colors add life to a landscape design. I often use purple, magenta, and pink—for every hue can be found in nature—and I consider no color off-limits. Once a student used fuchsia sprinkled with yellow dots for a sky, and it looked fabulous. Color choice is a personal thing, and my color taste may not echo yours. However, I encourage you to keep your color range broad. No fabric stash is balanced without a bit of lime green and orange in it!

A creative fabric stash develops when you buy fabric from a variety of sources. Try looking in dressmaking and window-treatment shops. Drapery fabrics offer unique designs and, while they're often heavier than the fabric we quilters tend to use, you can find reasonably lightweight drapery cottons to add a fresh look to your work. Always remember that the fabric market changes rapidly, sometimes two and three times a year, and a favorite from last year might never be found again.

*Even fabric that seems unrelated to a landscape, such as the fish fabric shown here, may yield some lovely landscape elements. And yes, my fabric stash has lots of pieces with the middles cut out—somehow that's always where the best part is!*

*Commercial fabrics*

*Batik fabrics*

Throughout the book I offer ideas and methods for altering commercial fabrics with colored pencils, oil pastels, and paint sticks to expand the possibilities. Fabric is a material to serve your artistic ideas and to adapt in as many ways as you wish with paint and other embellishments.

## Sheers and Specialty Fabrics

I use mainly cotton fabrics for my landscapes, but to add visual interest and texture I also incorporate silk, satin, tulle, tissue lamé, printed lace, organza, and metallic fabrics. The luster of silk and satin makes them wonderful choices for sky and water. Their reflective quality brings a feeling of light and vibrancy to the landscapes.

Quilters tend to avoid silk and synthetics, but it's possible to work these fabrics into your art quilts and landscapes if you simply learn the proper techniques. Fusible appliqué is one such technique that opens up many possibilities for working with difficult fabrics such as taffeta, silk, and polyester. I always look forward to prom season and its new crop of interesting fabrics for gowns: prismatic tissue lamé, silks, and many different types of sheers have all danced their way into my landscapes. You'll learn how to use sheers to add textural richness. In the little landscape on page 11, called "Fence," I frayed the edges of sheer fabrics and stitched them into place with small running stitches.

### Less Is More

This landscape, made by a student in one of my workshops, displays a courageous use of fabric. It's simple, containing just eight separate pieces, yet conveys so much through its use of color and print. Miles of vivid canola fields and the scale of distant grain elevators evoke the expansive prairies. The dramatic sky fabric balances the almost overpowering yellowish orange. Maxine used the reverse side of a Japanese woodblock print and it poetically expresses a lashing thunderstorm—an unexpected and clever way to use the language of the cloth. A powerful sense of place is packed into these few fabrics. This is, simply, good design.

Prairie Storm *by Maxine Robertson, 6½" x 4½"*

## Hand-Dyed and Painted Fabrics

I don't dye much fabric of my own, as so many other quilters make beautiful hand-dyes and I love buying their products. Hand-dyed fabrics have a soft, painterly watercolor look that's very effective for landscapes. I particularly like using hand-dyed and hand-painted fabrics for sky. (Mickey Lawler paints especially beautiful land and sky fabrics, which are available from Skydyes. See "Resources" on page 96 for information.) Nowadays there are many commercially printed fabrics that look like hand-dyed fabric. Most of the dye painting I do is with the Ranger Heat Set Ink iron-on dyes on satin for sky and water, and also for coloring organza and sheers. You'll learn this iron-on method of dyeing satin in the project "Spring Comes Softly" on page 49.

## Fabric Preparation

The landscape projects are either framed or intended as wall hangings. They won't be subjected to the stresses usually sustained by a quilt, so you needn't follow the traditional quiltmaker's rules for preparing fabric. Washing fabrics is not necessary, and I also pay little attention to the grain of the fabric. I do keep my fabric ironed, as pressed fabric is ready to audition and easier to cut accurately. However, if you plan to incorporate small landscapes into a quilt or garment that will be subjected to the stresses of wear and washing, please follow the standard rules of washing the fabrics, and pay attention to the grain line when cutting out landforms.

## FINAL THOUGHTS ON FABRIC

I suggest that you study the fabric choices in the photographs of projects throughout the book. Then revisit your own fabrics with a viewfinder and a fresh eye to see what landscape elements they reveal. I'm sure you'll come up with some exciting finds. If that fails, well, you will just have to go fabric shopping!

Fence *by Valerie Hearder, 3¾" x 5"*

*Sheers and specialty fabrics*

*Hand-dyed fabrics*

If you sew or quilt, you probably already have most of the supplies needed for making landscapes. There may be a few things that you'll need to gather up from other areas of your house and some items that you'll need to purchase to have on hand.

## Cutting, Measuring, and Marking

- Rotary cutter, cutting mat, and gridded ruler (a 6" x 14" ruler is a good size for landscapes)
- Scissors for fabric, scissors for paper
- Pins and needles
- Craft knife
- Chalk liner or other fabric marker
- Pencils, fine-point black marker, ruler
- Tracing paper
- White copy paper

## Sewing

- Fabrics: cotton, muslin, silk, tulle, organza, polyester satin
- Beads
- Cotton or cotton-covered polyester thread for hand and machine sewing
- Rayon, embroidery, and metallic threads for decorative stitching
- Cotton batting

## Fusing, Pressing, and Stabilizing

- Nonstick pressing sheet such as Teflon or parchment paper
- Fusible webs for adhering and stabilizing appliqué shapes. Brand names include: Wonder Under (paper backed), Steam-a-Seam (paper backed), and Misty-Fuse (without paper)
- Stabilizers:

  Sulky Totally Stable iron-on stabilizer, for machine embroidery

  Sulky Heat-Away vanishing muslin

  Sulky Fabri-Solvy heavyweight water-soluble stabilizer

  Lightweight dressmaker's iron-on interfacing
- Iron cleaner such as Dritz Hot Iron Cleaner

## Coloring Fabrics

- Transfer dyes such as Ranger Heat Set Inks
- Oil paint sticks such as Shiva Paintstiks
- Colored pencils such as Prismacolor
- Fabric crayons such as Crayola
- White copy paper, freezer paper
- Paintbrushes

## Mounting and Framing

- Masking tape
- White artist's tape
- Removable clear adhesive tape (optional)
- Backing board such as acid-free vellum, Bristol board, or museum board
- Mat frames, custom cut

*A selection of silk, rayon, and metallic threads, beads, and braids in my sewing basket*

In this section I discuss the key pattern and construction elements that are common to all the projects. Put these into practice by making the simple "Basic Landscape," which will give you a solid grounding for all the other projects. You can then proceed sequentially, project by project, to learn each new technique, or jump to the landscapes that catch your fancy. The supplies list for the "Basic Landscape" will be referred to in the instructions for the other landscapes. If you want to expand on the basic project, a quick look through the book will give you many ideas for embellishing it. Be sure to read about fabric choices on page 8 before beginning your project.

## WORKING PAPER FRAME

Framing is a key element of these landscapes, and many of the projects require a working paper frame to help define the landscape and to serve as a bridge to the final mat in which the landscape will be mounted. Make a simple frame from white paper, with an opening cut to match the finished size of your project. Lay the paper frame over the landscape while it's being composed to show the size of the finished piece and help you visualize the proportions of the design. Use the working frame until the finished piece is ready to be taped into a custom-cut mat frame or until you attach a fabric border. You can also use the paper frame like a viewfinder to help you choose the most effective part of the fabric.

When the finished size of a framed landscape is given in the project directions, it refers to the area defined by the window in the mat frame, not the outside edge of the mat. When a landscape is finished with fabric borders and binding, no paper frame (or mat) is used. Details on mounting and framing begin on page 31.

## THE MUSLIN BASE

The muslin base serves three functions. It is a size guide for cutting and placing each fabric piece, a foundation for all the separate pieces of fabric to lie on, and, when the composition is complete, a base to pin the pieces to. The muslin base is ½" larger on each side than the opening of both the working frame and the mat frame. This ½" extension beyond the frame line is the margin needed to mount the landscape into the mat frame. Don't pin the pieces to the muslin base until all the pieces have been positioned in the landscape.

## PLACEMENT GUIDE

Use a fine-point marker to trace the landscape pattern onto tracing paper for a placement guide. There is no need to mark numbers or the dotted lines on this copy, but do include the frame line. This pattern is kept intact and is laid over the landscape to check the positioning of each piece within the composition. The placement guide is also helpful for minor adjustments that may be needed when you stitch the landforms in place and again in the final stage of mounting the landscape in the mat frame.

## TEMPLATE PATTERN

The template pattern is your guide to cutting out each landform piece. Trace the pattern onto tracing paper including the dotted lines and numbers. Before you use the template pattern, trim to the line representing the outside edge of the muslin base. The dashed lines in the pattern represent the additional allowance needed on the sides and bottom of each landform piece that will be cut from fabric. Cut the landform big enough to cover the muslin base and to provide an underlay for the next fabric piece. Each landform piece extends beyond the frame line by ½" (the frame margin) to the edge of the muslin base. As you construct the landscape, cut away each numbered pattern piece from the template pattern, in sequence, and discard. The top edge of the remaining template pattern is used to mark the cutting line of the next numbered piece onto the fabric.

A delightful part of making landscapes is finding the perfect part of a fabric to suggest a hill, valley, or sun sparkling on water. Because the template pattern is translucent tracing paper, you can position it over the fabric and move it around to choose the best part of the fabric print for the shape you are about to cut out.

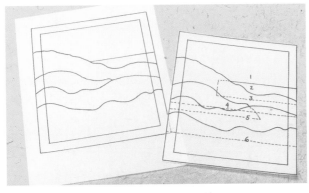

*The placement guide is on the left and the template pattern is on the right. Trim the excess paper from the edges of the template pattern.*

## SEAM ALLOWANCE

Some of the landforms are hand appliquéd in place; the necessary seam allowance for hand appliqué is included in each pattern piece. When marking and cutting the landform pieces, don't add extra for turning under. Position each piece in the landscape exactly as shown in the pattern. When you stitch the landscape, each piece is turned under approximately $1/8$", which is sufficient for needle-turn hand appliqué. Any machine sewing for borders is done with a $1/4$" seam allowance.

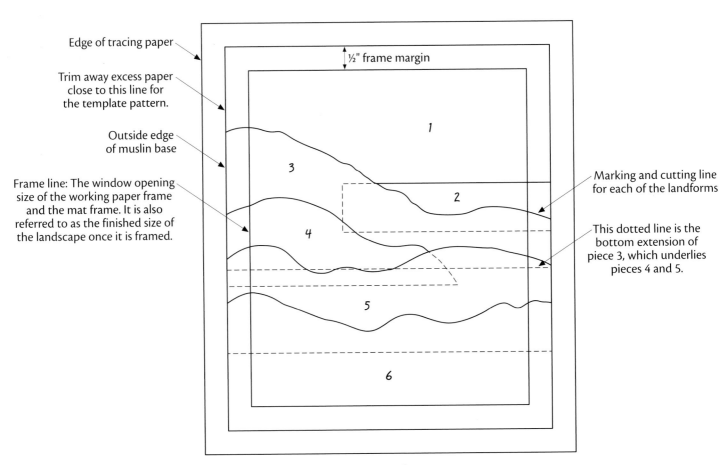

**Pattern key**

PATTERN AND CONSTRUCTION METHODS

# THE BASIC LANDSCAPE

## MATERIALS

*All scrap sizes are approximate.*

7" x 8" piece of muslin for base

Fabric scraps:

　1 piece, 4" x 8", for sky

　1 piece, 3" x 6", for sea

　4 pieces, 4" x 8", for hills

Basic supplies:

　1 sheet of white paper, 8½" x 11", for working frame

　2 sheets of tracing paper, 8½" x 11"

　Black, fine-point marker

　Ruler, craft knife, small paper scissors

　Fabric marking pencil

Mat frame

## MAKING THE LANDSCAPE

1. Make a working frame from a sheet of white paper. Using the ruler and marker, draw the opening 6" wide and 7" high. It doesn't have to be dead center on the sheet. Use the craft knife and ruler, or paper scissors, to cut away the window in the working frame. This window is the finished, framed size of the landscape.

2. Lay the muslin base on a table in preparation for placing the cut pieces.

3. On tracing paper, make two copies of the pattern on page 19, one to use for the template pattern and the other for a placement guide. Trim away the excess paper from the edge of the sheet that will be used for the templates. Refer to "Placement Guide" and "Template Pattern" on page 13 for details.

4. Cut the sky fabric (pattern piece 1) to 3¼" x 7" and the sea fabric (pattern piece 2) to 1¼" x 4¼". A ¼" seam allowance is included in these measurements for joining the two pieces.

Ocean View: September
*by Valerie Hearder, 6" x 7"*

5. Lay the sea and sky pieces together, right sides facing, being sure that the sea piece will be joined to the lower-right edge of the sky. Using a ¼" seam allowance, stitch the sea and sky together by machine to create a nice, straight horizon line (fig. 1). Press toward the sea piece. Lay the unit across the muslin, aligning the top edges (fig. 2). This creates the background on which you will compose the hill shapes.

6. Carefully trim away pieces 1 and 2 (sky and sea) from the template pattern. Next, choose fabric for hill piece 3. Lay the template pattern on the fabric, being sure to choose the best part of the fabric print for the hill shape. There is no need to worry about grain line. With a fabric marking pencil, draw the cutting line by following the top edge of piece 3 and down each side line (fig. 3). The dotted lines at the bottom of the piece show you how deep it needs to be cut. This is the allowance for the next shape to overlap.

7. Cut out shape 3 along the marked lines. Lay it down on the sea-and-sky unit, but don't pin any pieces to the muslin until they are all in place (fig. 4).

8. Trim away piece 3 from the template pattern. Choose the next fabric and mark the top edge and left side of piece 4 on the fabric (as you did in step 6). Lift the template pattern and refer to it to mark the right side and bottom extension lines on the fabric (fig. 5). Cut out the piece and place it in the landscape composition (fig. 6).

9. Trim away piece 4 from the template pattern. Lay the remaining pattern on the next fabric and mark the cutting lines for piece 5 (fig. 7). Cut it out, and lay it over pieces 3 and 4 (fig. 8). Note that for this shape, I lined up the dashed line for the bottom of the piece with a straight edge of the fabric (fig. 7). You should place the pattern in the best position on the fabric and then cut it out, allowing for the area to be overlapped. You may need to lift up the pattern as you did in step 8 to mark the cutting line for the bottom.

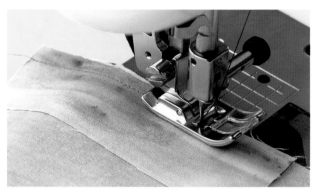

Fig. 1. Stitch the sea and sky piece together using a ¼" seam allowance.

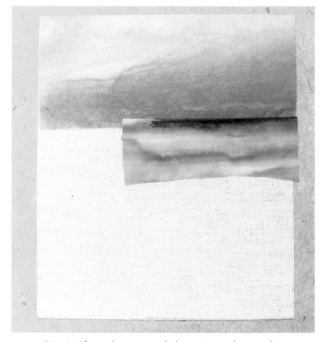

Fig. 2. Place the sea and sky unit on the muslin, aligning the top edges.

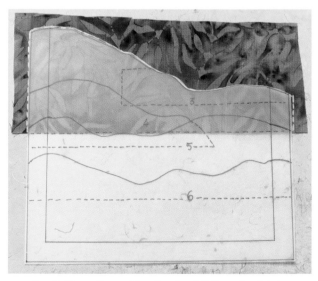

Fig. 3. Draw the cutting line for hill 3 on the fabric.

Fig. 4. Position the hill shape on the sea and sky unit.

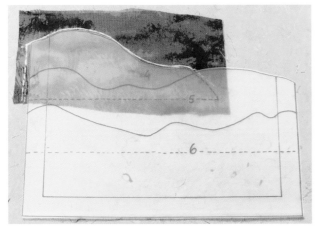

Fig. 5. Draw the cutting line for hill 4 on the next fabric.

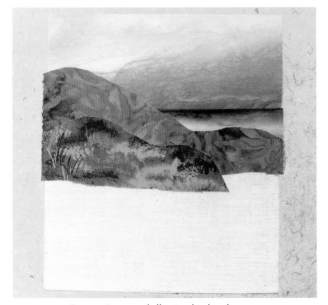

Fig. 6. Position hill 4 in the landscape.

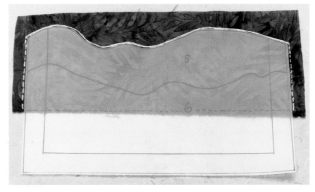

Fig. 7. Mark the cutting line for hill 5.

Fig. 8. Position hill 5 in the landscape.

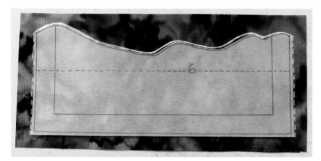

*Fig. 9. Mark the cutting line for hill 6.*

10. Cut piece 5 away from the template pattern, mark the cutting lines for piece 6 on the remaining piece of hill fabric (fig. 9), and cut out shape 6. Position it across the bottom of the landscape (fig. 10).

11. Lay the pattern you traced for a placement guide over the landscape and adjust all the pieces to match the pattern lines (fig. 11). It's fine if the pieces are cut and placed slightly different from the pattern. If it looks good to your eye, that's what counts. Small changes are part of the process and add your own touch to the design.

12. Set the placement guide aside and place the paper frame over the landscape. Check that the water horizon line is horizontal and parallel with the top edge of the paper frame.

13. When each piece is positioned correctly, slip a piece of sturdy paper or a file folder under the muslin base to carry it to the ironing board, and then press with a dry iron. Next, pin everything in place, spacing pins about 1¼" apart. I prefer ¾" appliqué pins because they are fairly short and are not likely to tangle the threads when I'm hand stitching. Don't pin too close to the cut edges, as you need room to turn under the edges when you sew them. The landscape is now ready to sew together using hand appliqué. Refer to "Needle-Turn Appliqué" on page 20.

14. When stitching is complete, gently press the landscape using steam.

15. If you plan to mount and frame your piece, lay the paper frame on the landscape and pin it in place as a size and placement reference for the mat frame (fig. 12). See "Mounting and Framing" on page 31 for details. If you plan to make a quilted wall hanging, see "Quilt Finishing" on page 34.

*Fig. 10. Position hill 6 in the landscape.*

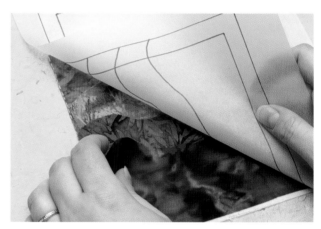

*Fig. 11. Make adjustments to the pieces with the help of the placement guide.*

*Fig. 12. Pin the paper frame in place on the landscape.*

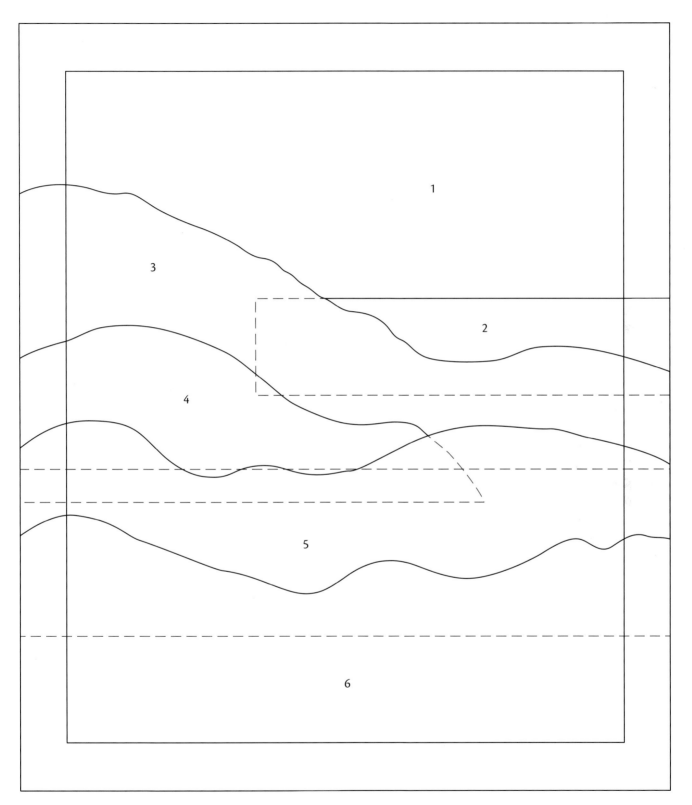

**Basic landscape pattern**

Appliqué—both fusible appliqué and hand appliqué—is at the heart of these landscape projects. If you want to create your entire landscape using fusible appliqué, that's just fine. But sometimes I adore the restful rhythm of hand appliqué as the needle dips in and out of the cloth while I sit and sew. These little landscapes stitch up quickly and the somewhat stippled line of careful hand stitches is a loving testament to handwork. When I do hand appliqué, I use the needle-turn method and a blind stitch.

There is no single right way to appliqué and no immutable rule that says your stitches have to be invisible, so use whatever appliqué method you're comfortable with. A slanting row of visible stitches outlining a hill shape adds texture. A row of little running stitches along a raw edge can add a soft, diffused feeling to the landscape. You could even use a buttonhole stitch. Even if you haven't hand appliquéd before, give it a try and each piece will get easier. As with everything, practice makes perfect—but remember, it's the pleasure of the making that's important, not the perfection.

## NEEDLE-TURN APPLIQUÉ

The needle is the basic appliqué tool and the finer the needle, the finer the stitch. Some appliqué stitchers prefer silk thread, which glides through the fabric and seems to make invisible stitches. I don't have a strong preference, as long as it's a fine thread and doesn't tangle too much as I stitch. What's most important is to match the thread color to the piece that is to be stitched down, not to the background fabric. So, if you are stitching a green hill to pink sky, use green thread.

The nature of textile landscapes generally involves soft, undulating curves. Curves cut on the bias swoop under easily with the needle-turning technique and won't need to be clipped or notched, as is the case for deep, sharp V shapes. As I sew each landform in place, some stitches go through to the back and catch the muslin base, and

some stitches don't, which is fine. The muslin has served its main purpose as a base to hold everything together and once I start stitching, I don't give it another thought.

The landscape patterns are numbered starting with 1 for the sky, at the top, with successive pieces layered and numbered toward the foreground, or bottom. The pieces are then stitched in the same sequence as you laid them down. The basic appliqué principle is: whatever touched the background first gets sewn down first. If you appliqué the foreground first, the pieces will become bunched up and out of alignment. Keep the placement guide handy while you stitch so you can reposition pieces as necessary.

I seldom trim away the hidden layers that build up under the multiple pieces in the landscapes. This step simply is not necessary for a project that is to be a wall hanging or framed piece. However, if you are incorporating the landscape into a quilt or garment, I do suggest you trim away the hidden layers to reduce bulk. Trim after each shape is stitched into place. Iron the piece, and then lift it and cut away the underneath layer.

My preference is to press the completed appliqué landscape with a steam iron. I press gently in an upward motion, toward the sky piece. This pushes up each hand-appliquéd edge slightly and hides the blind stitch even more. The ironing gives each shape a crisp edge and adds definition to the landscape. If you prefer a puffy, dimensional look to your appliqué, don't press it. Remember, if you've used synthetic fabrics in the landscape, such as tulle or metallics, use a pressing sheet to protect both the fabric and your iron.

To appliqué a piece using the needle-turn method:

1.  Thread a fine needle—a size 10 or 11 Sharp is a good choice—with an 18" length of thread and knot the end. The thread color should match the appliqué piece that is to be stitched down. Hold the landscape in your left hand

and, starting at the right-hand side of the piece, use your thumb to firmly anchor the top edge of the piece. (Left-handed quilters should follow these instructions in reverse.) Sweeping the tip of the needle from left to right, turn a ⅛" seam under the thumb. Finger-press the fold with your thumb to make a crisp edge. Turn under and finger-press about ½" at a time, enough to allow for the next few stitches.

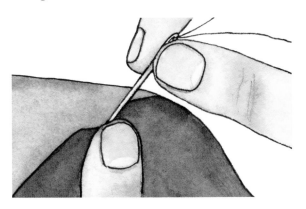

2. Keep your thumb firmly on the piece and bring the needle up from the back of the landscape, directly into the crisp, folded edge of the seam. The needle must go exactly into the folded edge and not into the surface of the piece—this is the key to a blind stitch. Pull the thread all the way through until it's taut. The knot will be on the back side of the landscape.

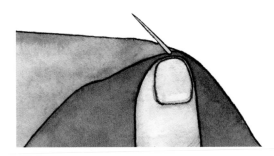

3. Dip the needle straight down into the background fabric, in the same spot where it came up (not ahead and not behind, as that would make a slanted stitch). The place where the thread comes through the folded edge of the top piece marks the spot for the needle to reenter the background fabric, ready to form the next stitch. When dipping the needle into the background fabric, tuck the needle tip

slightly under the top appliqué piece and push it through to the back. As the thread is pulled through to complete the stitch, it will pull the edge of the piece under slightly, helping to hide the stitch. Give the thread a gentle tug at the completion of each stitch to make it snug.

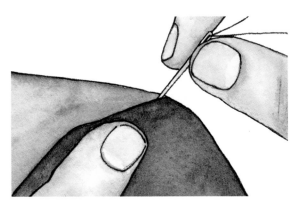

4. To form the next stitch, slide the needle through the background fabric, picking up about ⅛", and come up directly into the fold of the top piece, as before. The spot in the fold where the needle comes up is the marker for where the needle will go back down into the background fabric to begin the next stitch.

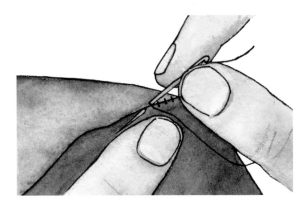

Remember to keep finger-pressing ahead of your stitching to keep a crisp fold. Continue with these steps, stitching from right to left, to the end of the piece. Finish by pushing the needle to the back side of the landscape. Make a few backstitches, and snip the thread.

There is no need to stitch all the way to the end of a piece if a top layer will cover the stitching. Fold back the top piece to expose enough of the underneath piece to stitch it in place for about an inch; then the top layer will cover it when it's stitched in place.

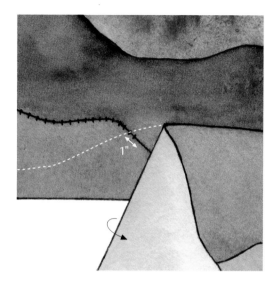

## MACHINE APPLIQUÉ

If you are a machine buff, you may choose to stitch the landscapes by machine rather than by hand. These projects will work perfectly for that because many layers are built up when composing the landscape, providing a firm base for machine stitching. The sky's the limit when choosing a machine stitch to appliqué the shapes. A satin stitch in a contrasting rayon thread gives a strong outline, echoing each landform shape, and adds to the rhythm of the design. Or perhaps try a narrow zigzag stitch with invisible thread. In "Land Rhythms" above right, which is all fused, I used a built-in appliqué stitch on my Brother sewing machine. It's a fine stitch that just catches the edge and gives each shape a pleasing stippled edge. Because all machines are different, make up a sample and experiment with the combination of thread, needles, and tension, making adjustments as needed.

## FUSIBLE APPLIQUÉ

Fusible appliqué is useful and very effective. I consider it a basic technique for landscapes. The process begins by ironing a fine web of glue to the back of fabric. This melted web stabilizes the fabric threads so that fine shapes can be cut out and the edges won't fray. The fused shapes are then applied

Land Rhythms *by Valerie Hearder, 4½" x 6½"*

onto another fabric by ironing in place. You'll find fusible appliqué used in most of the projects in this book, for everything from adding small details to fusing an entire landscape.

When small details are fused into place they seem to blend and become one with the fabric to which they're fused. A fused moon looks like an integral part of the sky without the raised edge that stitching would make. It's essential to use some sort of nonstick pressing sheet when working with fusible webs. A Teflon pressing sheet is an almost permanent fixture on my ironing board because I often fuse details in my landscapes. I like these sheets because they are durable and last through years of use. There are substitutes, such as parchment paper or the paper that comes with paper-backed fusible webs. In the project directions, I simply refer to a "Teflon pressing sheet" when a nonstick sheet is required.

There are many excellent fusible webs on the market, most of which are paper backed. Steam-a-Seam Light and Wonder Under are good choices. Even if a web has a paper backing, I still use a Teflon pressing sheet to avoid getting fusible web melted onto my iron. There is also a paperless web called Misty-Fuse. I use this a lot because it's the lightest-weight web on the market and is environmentally friendly—solvent free and recyclable. It's particularly good for landscape projects when you need to hand appliqué over fused pieces. Misty-Fuse must be used with a Teflon pressing sheet.

For landscapes, I generally fuse the web to the wrong side of the fabric, and then cut shapes from the fabric. You can also trace a pattern onto the paper side of the web first, cut it out loosely following the lines, fuse to the wrong side of the fabric, and then cut on the lines.

To appliqué a piece using fusible web:

1. Place a Teflon pressing sheet on your ironing board and lay the fusible web on the sheet with the fusible side facing up. Layer the fabric on top with the wrong side of the fabric facing the fusible web.

2. Fold the Teflon sheet over to completely cover the fabric. Press for about four seconds with a dry iron at a cotton setting. Allow to cool for a few seconds and then unfold the Teflon sheet and peel off the fabric, which now has the fusible web melted onto the wrong side. If you used a paper-backed fusible web, peel off the paper. The fabric is now ready to cut into any shape you need.

3. The golden rule is to keep the Teflon pressing sheet wiped thoroughly clean after every use—or you may end up ironing a glob of fusible gunk into your design. Use a small wad of cotton batting or fabric (not your fingernail or other sharp object) to wipe off every trace of fusible web that might remain on the Teflon. Check the soleplate of your iron for residue as well. This can be cleaned with a product such as Dritz Hot Iron Cleaner or with fabric-softener sheets that have been used in the clothes dryer.

## Technique Tips

- Drape a piece of clean muslin over your ironing board to ensure a fresh, fusible web–free pressing surface. This saves a lot of wear on the ironing-board cover, and muslin is inexpensive to replace.

- It's rather difficult to cut out a tiny shape and then try to adhere fusible web to the back of it. Instead, cut out a piece of fabric larger than the desired shape, apply the fusible web, and you'll find that it's easy to cut fine details from the fused fabric.

- Paper-backed web is useful because you can fuse it to a piece of fabric and then draw the shape on the paper backing for an accurate cutting line. Or, since it is translucent, you can lay the paper-backed web on a drawing and trace the design onto the paper backing before fusing it to the fabric. Then it's easy to cut out an accurate shape following the tracing line. Remove the paper before fusing the shape into place.

- During the composition stage of the landscape design, I fuse pieces lightly with a low temperature setting on my iron. That way, if I change my mind, I can gently peel the pieces apart and reposition them. Only when 100% sure of the positioning will I use a hot iron for a full, permanent bond.

- If bubbles or wrinkles appear in a fused piece, it could mean that the iron was too hot or there was too much moisture. Wrinkles can often be ironed out. Or try peeling off the piece, ironing it again (using a Teflon pressing sheet, of course), and then reapplying it to the landscape.

- If you intend to use fusible appliqué in a quilt or a garment that will be subjected to washing and wear, I suggest machine appliquéing the edges of the fused shapes for durability.

The sky is a key atmospheric element that sets the tone of a landscape—a softly glowing sunrise, a gathering storm, or the clear bright blue of summer. Being able to create your own sky, water, or land-forms will add greatly to your landscape compositions and truly make them your own work of art. There are many excellent fabric paints, dyes, paint sticks, and fabric markers to choose from, and each one seems to inspire new ways of working with fabric. My criteria for fabric-coloring techniques are brief: they must be simple to use and nontoxic. All the paints and dyes I use in these projects are safe and can be used with children, if supervised. However, be sure to keep the products away from food-preparation surfaces.

I've designed four landscapes that incorporate iron-on transfer dyes, fabric crayons, oil paint sticks, and colored pencils. All of these are readily obtainable from craft or art-supply stores, or see "Resources" on page 96. But please experiment with whatever you can find or already have on hand. For example, you'll get good results from using regular artist's acrylic paint, which can be diluted and used on any type of fabric. You can also use school-grade colored pencils. When learning any new technique, experimentation is key. Try working with a number of sample pieces until you get the hang of the technique and are pleased with the results before starting your project. And finally, please remember that you can substitute your own painting techniques in any of these projects or simply use hand-dyed fabrics or commercial fabrics.

## IRON-ON TRANSFER DYES

I use Ranger Heat Set Inks, which come in 12 bright colors and can be softened into pastels with the addition of Ranger Textile Medium. Ranger Heat Set Inks were developed to re-ink stamp pads for rubberstamping. However, these "inks" are dispersed dyes that can be diluted and used to transfer images onto synthetic fabrics. You'll get the best results from 100% man-made fibers, or fabric with at least 65% polyester. I use white satin for its lustrous, reflective quality. It is especially lovely for water.

In addition to the inks, you'll need the following supplies:

- Newspaper to protect work surface
- Small jars (baby food jars are perfect) for mixing paints
- A bigger jar for cleaning brushes
- Watercolor brushes, sizes 8 to 12
- Paper towels

The basic technique for using transfer dyes is to paint the diluted dyes onto paper. Then, when dry, the painted side of the paper is placed onto fabric and ironed. I use good-quality copy paper for this technique, although almost any paper will work.

Paper will naturally buckle when wet, so the dye will tend to pool. Keep spreading the dye with your brush as it dries to eliminate pooled concentrations. When the painting is dry, I often apply a second layer of dye to create transparent layers of color. The dyes look dull and pale when they dry on the paper, but will magically transform into vivid color when ironed onto fabric. The painted paper must be bone dry or the dyes won't transfer.

To transfer the painting from the paper to the fabric, first protect your ironing board with some scrap fabric and place the paper, painted side down, onto your selected synthetic fabric. The key is to iron the paper transfer with the hottest iron possible without melting the synthetic fabric. Press with a heavy hand and keep the iron moving slowly for about a minute so the dye transfers evenly. If you hold the iron still, the outline of the iron will be transferred onto the fabric. This is especially noticeable when a row of steam vents appears in your sunset! Because the dye-painted paper is ironed face down onto the fabric, the transfer comes out in a mirror image. This is important to remember if you want a painted element to appear in a particular place in your creation, so anticipate the mirror effect when you are applying the dye to paper.

If your transfers come out too pale, it could be for one of three reasons: you did not press hard enough, the iron was not hot enough, or the dye solution is too diluted. The first two causes can be checked during ironing by lifting a corner of the paper, being careful not to shift or slide it, to see how well the paint is transferring. If the transfer appears pale, you can either turn up the heat on the iron (remembering to avoid a meltdown) or press harder. If the transfer is still too pale, add a few more drops of the Heat Set Ink to the dye solution and paint a new painting. The key is to experiment.

You can, of course, use the Ranger Heat Set Inks for rubberstamping as originally intended. Use them undiluted and rubberstamp a graphic image onto paper, wait for it to dry, and then iron the paper transfer onto your project as shown in the small sun-stamped landscape below. Just remember, the fabric needs to have at least 65% polyester content.

Sun *by Valerie Hearder, 2½" x 3½"*

### Technique Tip

Here is one of my favorite tricks. Gift-wrap paper and the decorative paper used by florists to wrap up flowers is printed with iron-on transfer dyes, so they work in the same way as the Ranger Heat Set Inks. This paper is a by-product of the fabric-printing industry and I usually find it in the grocery store floral department. Look for florist paper with leafy or floral patterns to cut out. The print on the paper has the characteristic dull look to it. Use a hot iron to transfer instant color to satin, organza, or mesh. You may get more than one print from the paper.

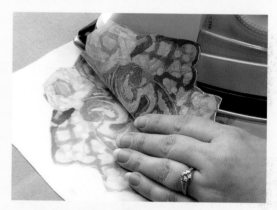

*Ironing florists' wrapping paper to satin*

## FABRIC CRAYONS

Fabric crayons work much the same way as the heat-transfer dyes, but in solid form. A crayon drawing is made on paper; the paper is then ironed face down onto synthetic fabric. I use white satin for my crayon transfers.

To get a good, strong transfer, lay down a thick, even layer of crayon on paper with no speck of white paper showing. Remove the little flecks of crayon that form while coloring—they will melt into dark spots when the drawing is ironed onto the fabric, or worse, they may fall onto your ironing board and be ironed permanently into other fabric. Your drawing will be in mirror image when you transfer it to the fabric, so allow for this when making your crayon transfer.

You can also use fabric crayons in combination with an iron-on transfer painting to add interesting textural elements, as I've done in the project shown below. Simply use the crayon to draw additional details, such as the grassy strokes shown, onto a dry transfer painting. Paper that has been colored with fabric crayons can also be cut up into shapes that can then be ironed into a composition to add a different texture—just be sure to iron them onto synthetic fabrics.

## OIL PAINT STICK

Oil paint sticks are like giant crayons in a thick cardboard sheath. They are oil paint in solid form. While a bit expensive, they last a long time. To use them, take a craft knife and remove the skin that forms over the paint tip. This skin preserves the volatile oils, keeping them from drying out.

The oils give off a slight odor when you first paint with them but they are permanent and odorless when they dry, which takes about 24 hours. Paint sticks are opaque and stand out well on dark fabric, particularly the iridescent colors of paint sticks, which are truly luscious. They do not have to be heat set if you are using them in a wall hanging—after all, they are designed for oil paintings. However, if you use paint sticks to decorate fabric that will be washed, heat setting helps to preserve their vibrancy.

## COLORED PENCILS

Colored pencils are a great addition to your box of tricks for coloring and making marks directly onto fabric that can then be stitched over for depth and texture. Think of them as a way to add pattern to the fabric. Colored pencils work beautifully to draw in details on a flower petal, add veins to a leaf, or add shading on a mountain to give the effect of hills. A white colored pencil is perfect for dusting a distant fabric mountain with snow. Generally, I prefer using colored pencils rather than fabric markers as I have more control with them

*A fabric crayon was used to achieve the look of grass on a background created by dry iron-on transfer painting.*

*Tropicana by Valerie Hearder, 6" x 7¼". Paint sticks were used to create the sun's rays in this vivid landscape.*

COLORING FABRIC

and can create finer or subtler details as desired. Prismacolor pencils are a good choice. They are mostly pure pigment bound in a wax base that melts when ironed, thus making the pencil permanent. I've also had good results from school-grade pencils, so experiment with any brand you have on hand. The marks made by colored pencils will not be subjected to laundering when used for the landscape projects in this book, but if you plan to use them in projects that might be washed, test for colorfastness first by washing a sample.

Watercolor pencils are another type of pencil worth trying out. Various brands, such as Caran D'Asche, are readily available from art-supply stores and can often be purchased singly if you want to play with a few colors to try them out. Use these to draw on fabric, and then add water with a paintbrush to blend the pencil marks, which dissolve into watercolor paints. Just remember that watercolor pencils work well for a wall hanging or framed landscape, but your drawings will disappear in the wash should you use them in a quilt.

In the example shown below, I created the look of the sun's reflection in the marshy water by using yellow and pink watercolor pencils. On the right side of the green fabric you can see the pencil marks, while the left side shows how the marks dissolved into watercolor effects when I added water with a paintbrush. I usually rub the wet pencil marks with my finger to help them blend.

## OTHER COLOR OPTIONS

Once you start experimenting with paints, dyes, and crayons of various types, you will want to try out more. Jacquard makes various types of user-friendly fabric paints that can be used straight from the jar and that clean up with water. Their shimmery metallic Lumiere paints are particularly lovely on dark fabric. Remember, when you are working with paints, dyes, and crayons, you'll achieve many random, surprising results—that is the charm of the medium. Use the landscapes in this book as a guide, without expecting to replicate them exactly.

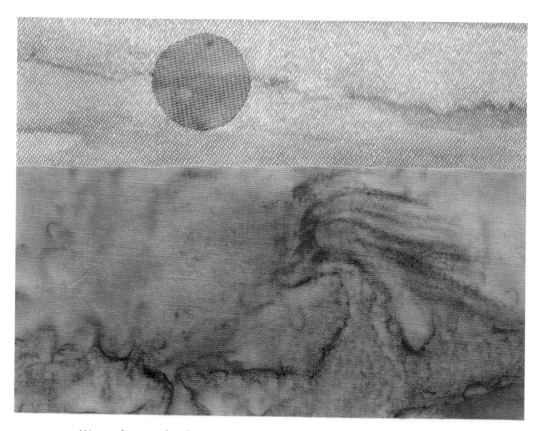

*Watercolor pencil is drawn onto fabric and then dissolved by adding water.*

My love of sewing and handwork began when I learned basic embroidery as a child, and I still have a soft spot for embroidery. Even a few embroidery stitches add a delightful touch to a landscape. Staying with my "simplicity" philosophy, I like to embellish landscapes with simple embroidery stitches. The nice thing is, I can easily pick them out if I don't like the effect. Beads, tulle, and netting marry beautifully with embroidery to add rich textural embellishment to a landscape.

I turn to whatever threads I have on hand to create the effect I want. I make fine stitches with a single strand of rayon thread to give the effect of grasses far away in the distance. For larger foreground stitches I use two or three strands of embroidery floss. Variegated threads are wonderful because they keep the color change subtle and interesting. A crewel needle is a good choice for hand stitching, but any fine needle will do the job.

I use just three basic stitches in most of my landscapes: straight stitch, French knot, and lazy daisy. The versatile straight stitch conveys beach grass, a fence rail, or small trees; French knots suggest pebbles, flowers, or a snowfall in the sky; and lazy daisy adds a tiny leaf or flower detail. Simple running and quilting stitches can also suggest contour lines or landscape features such as a furrowed field to add perspective and depth. Whole areas can be textured and shaded with embroidery stitches.

## STRAIGHT STITCH

This is the easiest stitch. Simply make random straight stitches of varying lengths and angles.

## FRENCH KNOT

1. Bring the needle up at A. Hold the needle close to the fabric and, keeping the thread taut, coil the thread around the needle two or three times.

2. Insert the needle down at B, very close to A but not in the same hole, while keeping the thread taut with the fingers of your free hand. You can change the size of the knot depending on how many times you coil the thread around the needle.

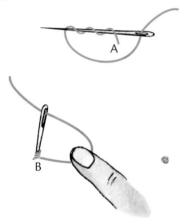

## LAZY DAISY

Bring the needle up from the back of the fabric at A. Form a loop with the thread and hold the thread down with your thumb. Insert the needle down at B (right next to A), and bring it out again at C. Pull the needle through, keeping the loop under the needle's point. Tie the loop down with a tiny stitch at D.

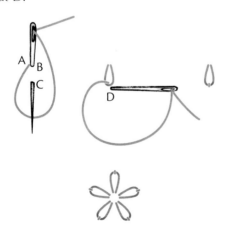

## BEADING

The beads that are stitched into a framed landscape or used as a wall hanging are not going to be stressed or subject to wear, so I don't worry about using special bead thread. I simply stitch the beads on with a double strand of embroidery floss. I like to use beads like strong spice—sparingly. A small sprinkling of fine beads goes a long way in a small-scale landscape. Also be aware of scale: large, clunky beads may look too heavy for a delicate landscape.

## MACHINE EMBROIDERY

The sewing machine is a wonderfully versatile tool for stitching and embellishing your landscapes. Instead of appliquéing by hand, you can stitch down any of the landform shapes with a narrow satin or zigzag machine stitch to add color and texture. You can also add free-motion embroidery to any part of a landscape; see the Design Ideas for "Shadowland" on page 58.

When I add machine-stitching details to a landscape, I prefer to use a removable iron-on stabilizer on the wrong side of the landscape as I find it less restrictive than an embroidery hoop. There are various brands of iron-on stabilizers available from fabric shops, and one I've used with good results is Sulky Totally Stable. This iron-on stabilizer holds the landscape taut, provides a firm base for the machine stitches, and prevents puckers. When the stitching is complete, I gently tear the stabilizer off the back.

*Rather than use an embroidery hoop, try stabilizing the back of your piece with removable iron-on stabilizer.*

Free-motion embroidery offers exciting options for embellishing a landscape, and it just takes a little practice to become familiar with the process. A hoop is often used to secure the fabric tightly, but I like working without the limitations of a hoop. If you've never done any free-motion work, prepare a practice piece by ironing a 12" square of fabric onto some stabilizer or stretching it in a hoop. It is essential that the fabric be held flat and taut while machine stitching. Refer to your machine's instruction manual under the category "darning" or "free-motion stitching."

Attach the appropriate darning or embroidery foot and lower the feed dogs. If you can't lower the feed dogs on your machine, tape a piece of cardboard over them so that your work can slide around in any direction under the needle without competing with the movement of the feed dogs. Set the stitch-regulator button to 0. The length of the stitch is controlled by how fast you move the fabric, balanced with how fast the machine is running. It's kind of like learning to drive a car with a standard transmission—you release the clutch at the same rate that you are pushing your foot on the gas pedal. Quickly you'll learn the balance and pace that makes for good, even stitches. A key to free-motion stitching is to take a deep breath, relax, and get into the flow of the stitches. It's important not to tense up and clench your hands—with a little practice you'll develop even stitches. Try making big, looping stitch patterns or writing your name in free-motion stitches.

## SPECIAL STABILIZERS

In "Fern Hill" on page 75, I used a special type of stabilizer called Sulky Heat-Away, also known as "vanishing muslin." This particular type of stabilizer is useful when stitching over an area that has no fabric base. For example, it is useful when stitching a fringe or edging, or for open work or lace work. It's a loosely woven heat-sensitive fabric that provides a firm base on which to machine stitch, and then disintegrates when pressed with a dry, hot iron. Never use steam with this product—in fact, water must never touch the vanishing muslin, or the chemicals in it may migrate to other fabrics and cause them to disintegrate when ironed. The vanishing muslin crumbles when heated and is easily brushed away, leaving just the stitches.

Confetti appliqué is another embellishment technique that requires a stabilizer. I used this technique for "Autumn Oak" on page 80. It makes wonderfully textured leafy trees and foreground shrubs. Layer tiny shards of sliced fabric between two pieces of water-soluble stabilizer and secure them with free-motion stitching. Soak the piece in water to dissolve the stabilizer and all you'll have left is the fabric and stitches. I use Fabri-Solvy from Sulky for my confetti appliqué because I prefer free-motion stitching without a hoop and this stabilizer is heavy enough to provide firm support. It dissolves quickly in warm water. Fabri-Solvy could also be used for the free-motion stitchery embellishment in "Fern Hill" on page 75.

### Technique Tip

Here is a neat trick to make a liquid stabilizer. Save all your Fabri-Solvy scraps and when you have the equivalent of about half a yard, put them in a jar with 4 ounces of warm water. This solution, which should be kept refrigerated, can be brushed onto any area that needs to be stabilized. Wait until it's dry, or use a hair dryer if you're in a hurry, and then stitch over the area. Dissolve the stabilizer by soaking the piece in water for a minute or two.

Standing Stones beyond the Bracken *by Penny Berens, 8⅜" x 6½"*

This exuberant landscape is based on a photograph of an avenue of standing stones in Dartmoor, England. Penny starts her landscapes with a thin batt cut to finished size and ironed onto a fusible stabilizer. The basic shapes are stitched over the batt by machine with raw-edge appliqué. Penny achieves depth by making the sky plain and flat. The middle ground has stab-stitch quilting, and the highly textured foreground evokes the coarse moor textures and stones with distressed burlap, velvet, and couched threads. Penny uses machine embellishment stitches to create frayed edges and simple straight-stitch hand embroidery for the standing stones. Hand-dyed cheesecloth is couched over cotton and wrapped around the edge.

In this section you'll find all the information needed for framing your landscape with an artist's mat. To finish your landscape using traditional quilting and binding, see "Quilt Finishing" on page 34. Mat framing is a way of presenting your landscape with impact and gives it a well-finished, artistic presence. For this reason, I suggest that you have a professional framer custom cut the mats for the projects in this book. When you make more landscapes of your own design, you may want to explore the ready-made mat frames on the market that are cut to standard sizes.

### Technique Tip

To protect your landscape from fading, whether it's framed or quilted, apply a thin layer of an acid-free UV spray such as Quiltgard Fabric Protector. It has a reputation for not harming fabric, and it helps preserve the fabric's color. It also keeps the landscape clean, should you decide to frame your landscape without glass. Spray the landscape either before you mount it in a mat frame or once the quilt binding has been completed and it's ready to hang.

## MATTING YOUR LANDSCAPE

When you are ready to visit the framer, pin the temporary paper frame over your landscape. The paper frame is the guide for how big to cut the mat's window opening. You can choose a single, double, or even triple mat. A double mat consists of two mat frames stacked one on top of the other. The top mat has a bigger window, cut to expose a narrow inner edge of the bottom mat. The bottom mat can be a different color and adds a nice accent line around the window.

Most quality mats are cut with a 45° beveled edge. This is to avoid casting a shadow on the artwork and it also looks more elegant than a straight edge. The top layer of the mat is made of colored paper and the core is usually white; however, colored cores are also available and provide an opportunity to add a thin accent to outline or blend with the landscape. You'll notice I've used black, blue, gray, pink, and green cores when matting the projects in this book.

Generally I try to choose acid-free mats for my landscapes. All paper mats will deteriorate over time and if conservation is a particular concern for you, use archival-quality mats made from cotton rag.

Choose the outside measurement of the mat to fit the size of hanging frame you want. I suggest you choose a standard outer dimension for the mat, enabling you to fit it into an inexpensive, ready-made frame. If you want to custom frame your landscape, a framer will have a good sense of what proportions to choose for your matted landscape. When the mat frame is cut, the next and final stage is to mount your landscape. There are two methods: taping or stitching.

## Mounting with Tape

Taping is a quick way to mount smaller work into a mat, and I've had good success with this method. I've used both masking tape and a white, acid-free artist's tape that's used for mounting watercolor paintings. A tape width of ¾" is sufficient.

1. Place the landscape face down on a flat surface. Cut a piece of tape the full length of the top edge of the landscape and press the tape across the top edge (on the wrong side), catching about ¼" of the landscape.

2. Flip the landscape over so that the tape is now sticky side up. Place the mat over the landscape, being careful to position it with the hori-

zon line straight, and then press it down so the mat sticks to the tape. The tape and edge of the landscape are behind the mat, as indicated by dotted lines.

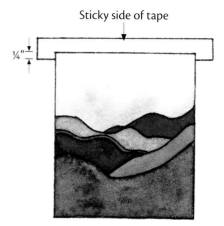

Sticky side of tape

¼"

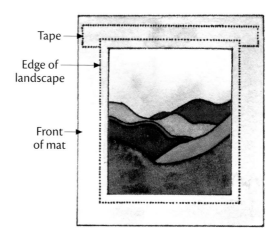

Tape —

Edge of landscape —

Front of mat —

3. Turn the mat over and press down hard on the tape so that it sticks well. Cut the next piece of tape and press it to the bottom ¼" (on the wrong side) of the landscape. Pull slightly to stretch the landscape and, keeping it taut, stick the tape to the mat. Remember: whenever stretching your landscape to tape it down, don't pull so hard that you stretch the stitches.

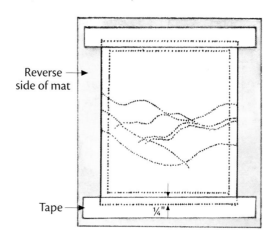

Reverse side of mat →

Tape →

¼"

4. Next, apply tape to first one side edge and then the other. Each time you tape an edge, pull it slightly to make the fabric nice and taut. When all four sides are taped, burnish the tape by rubbing it hard to make it stick fast to the mat frame—I use the handle of my scissors. To finish off the back, cut a piece of paper (I use ordinary white copy paper) big enough to cover the landscape and tape it down on all sides.

## Mounting with Stitches

The stitched method can be used for a landscape of any size, but it is especially useful for mounting landscapes bigger than about 8" x 10". It is also a firm way to mount landscapes that are heavily embellished and stitched. The machine stitching holds the landscape firmly and there is no danger of the landscape starting to come loose. It's also in line with good conservation practices. Jo Diggs kindly shared this method for mounting landscapes with me. The landscape is first taped and then stitched to a backing board that is taped to the mat frame. Use backing board strong enough to hold the landscape taut yet thin enough to machine stitch through. I bought an 11" x 14" pad of 100 lb., acid-free vellum Bristol board sheets that work well. They're available at art-supply stores. Alternatively, ask your frame shop for 2- or 3-ply museum board, or mounting board, preferably acid free.

1. Cut a piece of backing board 1½" bigger on all sides than the outer dimensions of your fabric landscape.

2. Center the landscape face up on the backing board and cut a strip of masking tape the same length as the landscape. Tape the top edge of the landscape to the board, catching about ⅛" of the fabric. Next, pull the landscape taut, without putting stress on the stitches, and tape the bottom ⅛" of the landscape to the board. The board may bend a bit, but will flatten when it's taped into the mat. Next tape the sides in the same manner, being sure to pull out any wrinkles or sagging areas.

MOUNTING AND FRAMING

3. Stitch the landscape to the backing board using your sewing machine. Choose a slightly longer stitch length on the machine and stitch the fabric just inside the tape. When all four sides are stitched, remove the tape.

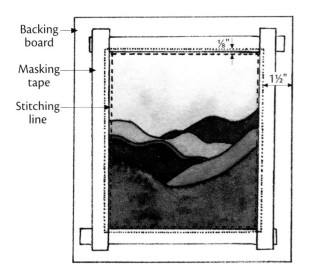

Backing board

Masking tape

Stitching line

⅛"

1½"

4. The placement guide used during the construction of the landscape is helpful here to place the finished landscape accurately into the mat frame. Be especially careful that any water horizon lines are parallel to the top edge of the mat frame. Place the backing board, landscape side down, on the table, and tape the top edge of the backing board with a strip of masking tape so that half of the tape sticks to the board and the other half is exposed.

5. Flip the backing board over so the landscape and the sticky edge of the tape are facing up. Place the mat frame over the landscape and carefully position it so the horizon line is straight; press down so the mat sticks to the tape. Turn the mat over, right side down, and finish taping each side of the backing board to the wrong side of the mat.

## Technique Tip

To get very precise placement of the landscape in the mat frame, lay the mat on the placement guide and put a small piece of removable tape on the mat to mark the alignment of the water horizon. Then, when you place the mat over the landscape, line up the horizon lines with the tape. Caution: Use only removable tape, as regular tape may damage the mat. Be sure to test first on the wrong side of the mat.

## SIGNING YOUR WORK

There is something wholly satisfying about adding your signature to your framed landscape. It's the finishing flourish and gives a sense of accomplishment. I sign my landscapes on the mat frame. Traditionally, paper is signed with pencil because graphite won't fade. But a metallic gel pen looks great on a dark mat, too! Another way to sign your work is to stitch your name or initials directly onto the landscape. You can add details about the landscape on the reverse side.

## FRAMING

Before you insert your matted landscape into the frame, you'll need to decide whether to use glass. There are two schools of thought on the subject. There are those who don't like to put glass over a textile because it bars the observer from the tactile nature of the medium—and then there are those who think glass is a good way to keep the project clean. I fall into the latter category. I also think a frame looks better with glass in it. I prefer clear glass, not the nonglare type that obscures the work. Ultimately, using glass is a personal preference and if you've added a protective spray to the fabric, you've taken a good step toward keeping the fabric clean without the use of glass. Whichever way you choose to display your landscape, please protect it from direct sunlight, which will damage the fabric.

For landscapes that will become small quilted wall hangings, you can use traditional quilting techniques to add borders, quilt, and bind. Refer to the following sections as needed when you finish the central design of your project.

## BORDERS

The wall-hanging projects include specific measurements and instructions for cutting the border strips for butted and mitered corners. A butted corner is the simplest method for attaching borders. Strips are stitched on either side of the quilt, and then the top and bottom border strips are stitched straight across the quilt, making squared corners.

Butted corners

## Mitered Borders

Mitered border corners are worth the little bit of extra effort involved as they add an elegant, framed look to the quilt. The 45° corners are hand stitched from the front instead of the back, and I always get accurate results. The steps that follow include instructions for determining the length to cut borders if you are designing your own quilt. The lengths needed for specific projects are given in the project directions.

1. To determine the length to cut border strips, work from the front of the quilt and measure the vertical sides. To that measurement add two border widths. Then add 4" so that the borders will extend an extra 2" at each end for mitering. For example, if the vertical side of the quilt is 20" and the border strip is 1½" wide, add 3" to the length, and then add 4". The border strip would be cut 27" long.

2. Cut the border strip and center it across the edge of the quilt, right sides facing and with the extra length of fabric extending at each end. Machine stitch the strip to the landscape with a ¼" seam. Repeat for the opposite side. Press the seam allowances toward the border.

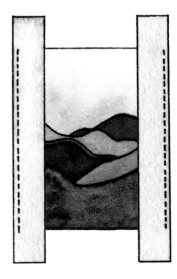

3. Measure the border strips for the top and bottom of the quilt, adding the extra length as described in step 1. Center the top strip on the edge of the quilt and machine stitch with a ¼" seam allowance, but here is the key: begin stitching exactly at the seam line of the side border. Use the flywheel of your machine to insert the needle as close to the edge of the

side-border seam line as possible. Stitch on the border and end your stitching exactly flush with the seam line of the other side border. Ending the stitching even one stitch away from the seam line will cause a gap when you fold back the top border to miter the corner. Repeat for the bottom border.

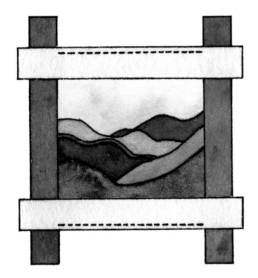

4. Press the top border open with the seam allowance toward the border. Fold the overlapping extension of the top border under itself, and pull it back until it forms a 45° angle over the underlying border, right sides together and lined up exactly with the edges.

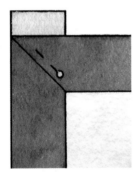

5. Press the miters and pin them in place. Thread a needle with a matching thread color and slip-stitch the miters in place on the front side of the borders. Try to make your stitches as invisible as possible. Turn the quilt over to the back and trim away the excess border extensions. Cut them on the diagonal, parallel to your hand stitching. Follow the same procedure for each corner.

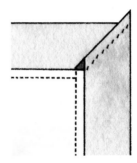

6. Once the borders are stitched, place the quilt on a cutting mat and use a large ruler to square up and trim the edges.

## QUILTING

Make a quilt sandwich with the backing and a layer of cotton batting. My favorite batting is Hobbs Organic cotton because it is a nice thickness for smaller pieces. Pin the layers together thoroughly and then add machine or hand quilting.

### Technique Tip

Spray baste the three layers together and you won't need to use pins. A basting spray, such as Sulky KK 2000, is temporary glue that dissipates after about four days. Spray a light coat onto both sides of the cotton batting and then layer it with the backing and the quilt top. Spray outdoors or spread newspaper down before spraying.

## BINDING

I like to use a narrow binding to complement the proportions of the small wall quilts. Four strips of binding are cut on the straight of grain, folded, and then machine stitched separately to each side of the quilt, overlapping the binding at each corner. Once you've sewn the binding on, slip-stitch the binding to the reverse side of the quilt.

1. Trim the quilt sandwich with a rotary cutter so the edges are even.

2. To determine the length of the binding, measure the side of the quilt and cut two 2¼"-wide strips to that length plus 1" for the overlap. Fold the strips in half, wrong sides together, and iron them. With the quilt face up, place the binding strips on opposite sides of the quilt, aligning the raw edges. Pin the strips in place and machine stitch with a ¼" seam allowance.

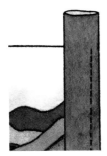

Front of quilt

3. Place the quilt face down on the ironing board and, on the back of the quilt, press the seam allowance toward the binding using a little steam. Now fold the binding toward the back of the quilt and slip-stitch it in place. Repeat for both sides. Lay the quilt on the cutting mat and use a rotary cutter to trim the extra length at the ends of the binding flush with the edge of the quilt.

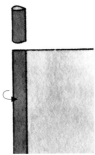

Back of quilt

4. Measure the top and bottom edges of the quilt to establish the length of the top and bottom strips, adding an extra 2". Cut two strips, 2¼" wide. Fold the strips in half, wrong sides together, and press. Machine stitch them to the top and bottom edges of the quilt front with a ¼" seam allowance. Each end will have a 1" extension.

5. Press the seam allowance toward the bindings as before, so that they lie flat. Trim the extensions to ½" longer than each end of the side of the quilt. Working on the back of the quilt, fold the ½" extensions of the bindings back over the raw edge of the quilt, and then fold the binding strip over and slip-stitch it in place to cover the machine stitching.

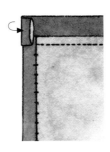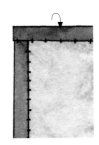

## HANGING SLEEVE

To display a wall quilt you will need a sleeve on the back to hold a hanging rod.

1. Cut a strip of fabric 5" wide and 1" shorter than the finished width of the quilt. Finish the ends of the strip by stitching a ½" hem. Fold the strip in half lengthwise, wrong sides together, and machine stitch it to make a tube. Press the tube so that the seam is centered on one side.

2. With the quilt face down, position the tube across the top edge of the quilt so the top of the tube covers the bottom half of the binding. Place the tube's seam against the quilt back to conceal it. Slip-stitch the tube to the quilt

back, taking care not to let your stitches show through to the front of the quilt.

## LABELING AND HANGING

As a way of signing your work, add a label to the back with the title, date, your name, the source of the pattern, and any other information you'd like to include.

Before hanging your quilt, read the Technique Tip on page 31. You may want to protect your landscape with Quiltgard Fabric Protector. Be sure to keep your landscape out of direct sunlight as well.

To hang the quilt, use a narrow dowel and put a small screw eye in each end. My favorite way to hang my quilts is to have a strip of Plexiglas cut 1" longer than the sleeve so that ½" shows out of each end of the sleeve but won't extend beyond the edges of the quilt. After a small hole is drilled in each extension, I can thread clear fishing line through the holes or place them over small finishing nails in the wall.

Waterloo County, Aerial View *by Renske Helmuth, 19¾" x 26¼".*
*Inspiration: an aerial photograph by Carl Hiebert.*

This wall hanging is machine quilted and made primarily from batik fabrics. Renske describes the freezer-paper method she uses for her landscapes: "Starting by enlarging an interesting picture, I lay a transparent overlay on the picture and trace the lines in with a black pen. I want as much detail as possible, but too many lines will make it look sloppy. The completed drawing is placed on the light table and a master copy is traced onto freezer paper. Each pattern piece is numbered, starting with 1 at the top. Piece 1 is then traced onto more freezer paper, cut out, and the fabric chosen and stitched in place on a background fabric. When piece 1 is appliquéd, that shape is then cut out of the master copy, so I can see how it looks. This procedure continues till all the pieces have been appliquéd and the master pattern is an empty rectangle."

# LATE AFTERNOON VIEW

BY VALERIE HEARDER ~ 11½" X 17½"

# I'm particularly fond of making detailed foregrounds, such as the leaf collage

in this landscape. It creates a sense of depth, as if the viewer is standing among the leaves watching the approaching dusk. Fusible appliqué is an ideal technique for creating fine details in a landscape. Once you start fusing you'll find many applications for it. Because this project has a stitched border and binding, the pattern has only a ¼" margin beyond the frame line. The gradated fabric that fades from light to dark in the borders adds to the atmosphere.

### FEATURED TECHNIQUE: FUSIBLE APPLIQUÉ

## MATERIALS

*Yardages are based on 42"-wide fabric. All scrap sizes are approximate.*

- ¼ yard of blue-and-pink fabric for outer border
- ⅛ yard of green fabric (3" x 30") for inner border
- 6½" x 8" piece of muslin for base
- Fabric scraps:

  1 piece, 4" x 8", for sky

  1 piece, 4" x 8", *each* of red, rust, purple, pink-and-yellow, and light green for hills

  1 piece, 3" x 6", of pale blue for water

  1 piece, 4" x 8", of checkerboard print for lower border

  Scraps of several leaf prints for collage

- 13" x 20" piece of fabric for backing
- ¼ yard of fabric for binding
- 13" x 20" piece of cotton batting
- Basic supplies (page 15)
- Teflon pressing sheet
- ⅛ yard of lightweight fusible web

## MAKING THE LANDSCAPE

Refer to "Pattern and Construction Methods" on page 13 and "The Basic Landscape" on page 15 for instructions as needed. *Note:* Pieces 2, 3, 4, and 5 are all fused to the background. Be sure to use a lightweight fusible web to avoid building up a thick layer of fused fabric when you hand appliqué piece 6 in place. Two layers of lightweight fusible web are a little stiff to stitch through by hand, but are still manageable.

1. Trace two copies of the pattern on page 43 onto tracing paper, one for the placement guide and one for the template pattern. Make a paper frame with an opening of 6" x 7½".
2. Cut sky shape 1 off the template pattern.
3. Cut the sky fabric to 3½" x 7" for piece 1 and lay it on the muslin base.

*Note:* Pieces 2, 3, 4, and 5 will all be fused. When you cut these shapes, they will be cut to the size indicated in the pattern. There is no extra seam allowance for turning edges under.

4. For shape 2, cut a 1½" x 3½" rectangle from the red fabric and from the fusible web. Fuse the web to the wrong side of the red fabric.

5. Place the template pattern on the right side of the red fabric, and use a fabric marking pencil to mark the top edge of shape 2. Cut it out and place it in the landscape, but don't fuse it into place until the composition is complete.

6. For water piece 3, cut a 1¼" x 4" piece from the pale blue fabric. (I used satin colored with transfer dyes as explained on page 24.) Iron a piece of fusible web the same size to the wrong side of the fabric using the Teflon pressing sheet. With a rotary cutter and ruler, trim the top edge to make sure it is straight and that there is no fusible web showing, and then place it over the lower edge of shape 2.

7. For shape 4, cut the rust fabric to 2½" x 5¼" and iron fusible web to the wrong side. Trim away shapes 2 and 3 from the template pattern and mark the top edge of piece 4 onto the fabric. Cut out and position the piece in the landscape composition.

8. For water shape 5, cut a 1" x 5½" piece from the pale blue fabric and iron fusible web to the wrong side. Trim the top edge with a rotary cutter and ruler and lay it across the bottom edge of shape 4.

9. Check the position of all the shapes carefully using the placement guide before fusing them in place. I suggest you work on your ironing board for this step as the pieces can easily shift out of place if you move the landscape.

10. Lay the paper frame over the landscape to check that the water pieces are parallel to the top and bottom edge of the frame. With a warm iron, press the shapes into place.

### Fuse Lightly First

An iron, set on low, will lightly fuse the pieces in place without forming a permanent bond. This allows you to gently peel the pieces apart to make small adjustments if needed. When you are sure of the placement, fuse the pieces with a medium-hot iron to make the bond permanent.

11. Cut away shapes 4 and 5 from the template pattern and mark the top edge of shape 6 onto the purple fabric. Position shape 6 in the composition. Pieces 6, 7, and 8 will be hand appliquéd. To compensate for the edge that will be turned under during appliqué, shift shape 6 up about ⅛"; this ensures it will be in the correct position when it's appliquéd. The placement guide is helpful for these adjustments during the stitching phase.

12. Cut away piece 6 from the template pattern and mark the top edge of piece 7 onto the pink-and-yellow fabric. Cut it out and arrange it in the composition.

13. Cut away piece 7 from the template pattern, mark the top edge of shape 8 onto the light green fabric, and cut it out. This piece will be the background for the collage of fused flowers and leaves.

14. Check the placement of all the landscape pieces using the placement guide and paper frame. Remove pieces 6, 7, and 8. Cover the landscape with a cotton pressing cloth and press pieces 1 to 5 into place with a medium-hot iron. Pin pieces 6, 7, and 8 into place and hand appliqué them. Press the hand-appliquéd pieces.

15. There is no pattern for the flowers and leaves since the composition depends on the fabrics you choose. Combine three or more different leaf and flower fabrics for interest. I used 3 different fabrics and 11 separate shapes for this collage. Cut out your leaf and flower shapes with a ½" cutting margin. Iron fusible web to the wrong side of each piece, and with small, sharp scissors, cut out the separate leaf and flower elements. Be sure to trim all edges so no fusible web shows. Play with the elements, referring to the pattern as you wish, to form a pleasing composition that will fit on piece 8. The collage must extend to the bottom edge of piece 8. When you are satisfied with the collage, use the paper frame to check the placement. Slip a piece of sturdy paper under

the landscape and transfer it to the ironing board. Press with a medium-hot iron to fuse the collage in place. Trim and square up the landscape, if necessary, so that it measures 6½" x 8".

16. Cut a 2" x 6½" rectangle from the checkerboard print and machine stitch it to the bottom of the leaf collage with a ¼" seam. Press the seam toward the checkerboard print.

17. From the green inner-border fabric, cut one strip, 1" x 6½", and two strips, 1" x 10". Sew the shorter strip with a ¼" seam to the top of the landscape and press toward the green. Sew a longer strip to each side and press.

18. From the blue-and-pink border fabric, cut a 6" x 7½" rectangle and stitch it across the bottom of the checkerboard print. For the outer borders, cut one strip, 2½" x 15", for the top and two strips, 2½" x 20", for each side. Referring to "Mitered Borders" on page 34, sew on the borders, mitering the top two corners.

19. Layer the landscape top with batting and backing. Quilt as desired. I added a satin-stitch accent line to the border using pale lavender rayon thread.

20. Refer to "Binding" on page 36 to bind and finish your quilt.

## Design Idea

If you can't find leaf fabric to cut out, make your own leaves from green fabric. Fuse the fabric to paper-backed web, draw the leaf shapes onto the paper backing, and cut them out. Draw leaf veins directly onto the fabric with colored pencils or fine-point fabric markers. Another option is to use realistic-looking silk leaves that make fabulous fusible appliqués. First, peel them off the plastic stems. Add fusible web to the wrong side, carefully trim away the fusible edges, and then fuse the leaves into place. Silk leaves are especially effective when combined with leafy prints of commercial fabric, as shown here.

## Technique Tip

Even with a Teflon pressing sheet and great care, you'll probably find traces of fusible web melted onto the soleplate of your iron. Check the soleplate often and clean with a wad of cotton batting or a used fabric-softener dryer sheet. If the fusible web is burned on, a product such as Hot Iron Cleaner will do the trick.

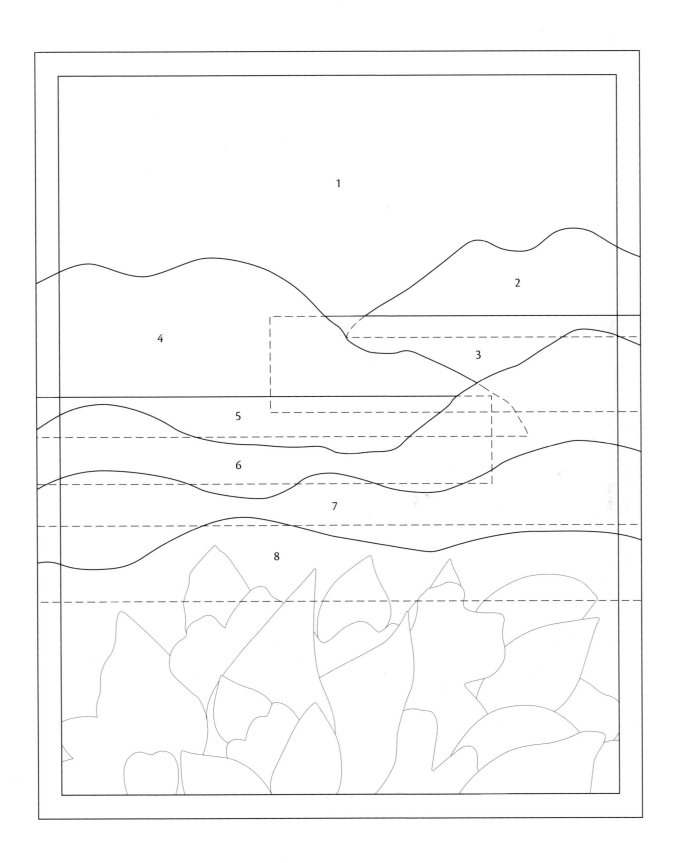

LATE AFTERNOON VIEW

# BLAZING HALO

BY VALERIE HEARDER ~ 6" X 7"

**The highlight of this simple landscape** is its rich sky with rays that spiral out from the sun like a halo. I used a brightly dyed piece of silk for the sky and added layers of tulle to create depth and subtle tonal variation, as well as to soften the bright colors. The fusible-appliquéd sun rays and hand quilting over the tulle with gold thread add another layer of embellishment. The combination of these simple elements and dark landform shapes makes for an atmospheric and complex-looking landscape.

**FEATURED TECHNIQUE: LAYERING TULLE**

## MATERIALS

*All scrap sizes are approximate.*

- 7" x 8" piece of muslin for base
- Fabric scraps:

  1 piece, 5" x 8", for sky

  1 piece, 5" x 8", *each* of gold lamé and orange for sun

  1 piece, 5" x 8", of yellowish peach for sun rays

  1 piece, 5" x 8", *each* of purple and blue for hills (4, 5)

  1 piece, 5" x 8", of plum for land (6)

  1 piece, 5" x 8", of gold stripe for grass
- Tulle scraps:

  1 piece, 6" x 7", *each* of navy, lavender, hot pink, and black
- Basic supplies (page 15)
- 8" x 10" piece of fusible web
- Teflon pressing sheet
- Gold thread
- Mat frame

## MAKING THE LANDSCAPE

Refer to "Pattern and Construction Methods" on page 13 and "The Basic Landscape" on page 15 for instructions as needed.

1. Trace two copies of the pattern on page 48 onto tracing paper, one for the placement guide and one for the template pattern. Make a paper frame with an opening of 6" x 7".

2. Cut the sky fabric to 4½" x 7" and lay it down on the muslin base. Cut out random cloud-shaped pieces from the colored tulle and layer them in place on the sky fabric.

### Taming Tulle

Working with small pieces of tulle is like working with slippery fish—they move around as you position each new piece. Ironing the tulle with a warm iron to flatten it goes a long way in making it behave.

3. When the tulle pieces are in place, cut a 5½" x 7" piece of tulle (I used purple) and lay it over all the smaller tulle pieces to hold them in place on the sky fabric. Press with a warm iron and pin the layers in place. Machine stitch the top piece of tulle to the outside edges of the sky fabric to secure the tulle to the sky fabric. Trim away the excess tulle around the outside edge and remove the pins.

*Layers of tulle create depth and tonal variation.*

4. For sun shapes 2 and 3, cut two 2½" x 3½" pieces of fabric. (I used shiny, translucent tissue lamé for 2, and orange for 3.) Iron fusible web to the wrong side of each piece. Cut away sky shape 1 from the template pattern and use it to mark the outline of sun shape 2 onto the fused side of the shiny fabric, including the dotted extension lines. Cut it out and set aside.

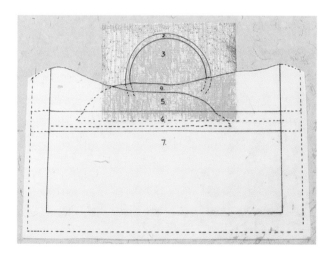

5. Trim away shape 2 and repeat the procedure for orange shape 3. Iron the sun shapes together, with piece 3 on top of piece 2, so they form one unit. (Be sure to use a Teflon pressing sheet.) Place this sun unit on the tulle-covered sky. Place the paper frame over the landscape and use the placement guide to position the sun unit. Keep the paper frame in place while you cut curved sun-ray shapes. These can be freehand shapes, echoing the cutaway arches of the leftover fused sun fabric that you used for shapes 2 and 3. As you cut, improvise with your own shapes to add a personal touch. Make two or three curved shapes out of each sun color. Be sure to lay them with the fusible side down on the tulle-covered sky. Use the pattern guide for placement.

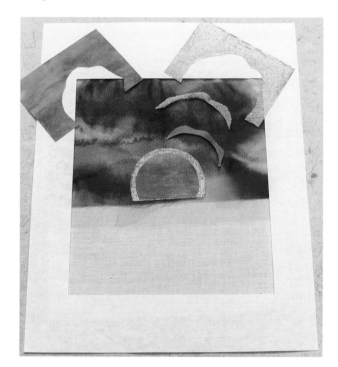

6. Cut a 5" x 5" square of yellowish peach fabric and iron fusible web to the wrong side. Cut off the corner to form a curve and then cut curved, wavy freehand strips to make the additional sun rays.

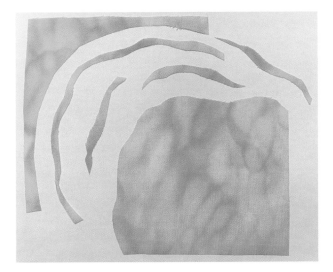

7. Cut and place wavy sun rays in the sky on top of the tulle until you have a pleasing composition. Cover the sky with a clean pressing sheet and, with an iron set on polyester (so as not to melt the tulle), press the fused pieces—the sun unit and halo rays—in place on the tulle. Pin the tulle again to make sure the tulle layers don't shift out of place during the rest of the construction process.

8. Cut away shape 3 from the template pattern and mark the cutting line for shape 4 on the purple fabric. Cut it out and place it in the landscape. Repeat for shape 5 using the blue fabric.

9. For piece 6, cut a 1" x 7" piece of plum fabric and place it in the composition. For piece 7, cut the gold-striped fabric to 2½" x 7". To add texture to the grassy look in my landscape, I frayed the top edge about ¼". Check the positioning of all the pieces using the placement guide and the paper frame.

10. Pin all the pieces in place and hand appliqué pieces 4, 5, and 6. Use gold or variegated metallic thread to add running hand stitches between the sun rays in the sky. These stitches also serve to anchor the layers of tulle. I left the top frayed edge of piece 7 loose and unstitched, but I machine stitched a few flowing lines with metallic thread to anchor it in place.

11. Mount the landscape in a mat frame, referring to "Mounting and Framing" on page 31.

### Design Idea

Various materials—sheers such as organza, slivers of metallic fabric, and decorative threads, for starters—can be layered under tulle to add sparkle and zip to your skies. Use black tulle to create a dark, stormy sky or add depth to landform shapes. Add beads or embroidery stitches to anchor the tulle and provide further embellishment. In the piece shown below, I placed ribbon and decorative threads under black tulle, and then anchored it with a large zigzag stitch. The foreground is a peacock feather.

### Technique Tip

A temporary spray glue such as Sulky KK 2000 or 505 Basting Spray (both nontoxic) is helpful when working with tulle. Spray the glue lightly onto the back of the piece of tulle and then smooth it into place in your landscape. The spray glue dissipates within a few days, leaving no residue. To make sure the spray is confined, spray the tulle inside a cardboard box.

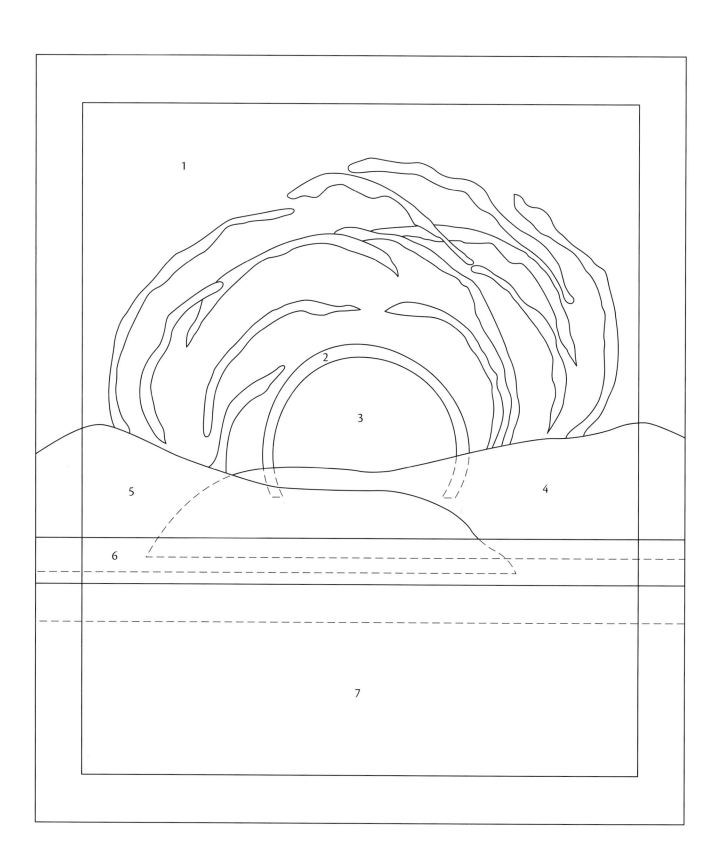

BLAZING HALO

# SPRING COMES SOFTLY

BY VALERIE HEARDER ~ 6" X 7½"

This landscape incorporates one of my favorite methods of creating skies and water—using Ranger Heat Set Inks. They are user-friendly, iron-on transfer dyes that are diluted and painted onto paper. The paper is then ironed onto synthetic fabric, such as satin, to transfer the color. While you have a batch of the dyes mixed, create a series of paintings for sky and water that you can use in other projects.

**FEATURED TECHNIQUE: TRANSFER DYES**

## MATERIALS

*Yardages are based on 42"-wide fabric. All scrap sizes are approximate.*

- ½ yard of white satin for sky and water
- 7" x 8½" piece of muslin for base
- Fabric scraps:

    1 piece, 5" x 8", of spotted batik for hill (2)

    1 piece, 5" x 8", *each* of 3 batiks for hills (3, 4, 6)

    1 piece, 5" x 8", of pale green for hill (7)

    1 piece, 5" x 8", of pale blue tree or leaf print for foreground (8)

- Scraps of tulle and organza: 2" x 5" pieces
- Basic supplies (page 15)
- Basic painting supplies (page 24)
- Ranger Heat Set Inks in purple, red, peach, blue, and yellow
- 10 sheets of copy paper cut into 4½" x 8½" pieces
- Teflon pressing sheet
- 7" x 7" piece of fusible web
- Mat frame

## PREPARING THE FABRIC

Refer to "Iron-on Transfer Dyes" on page 24 before you begin.

1. Protect your work surface with newspaper. Measure ⅛ teaspoon of each dye color into separate small containers. Add 3 tablespoons of water for each color and mix well with a paintbrush to dissolve the dye. Paint one 4½" x 8½" piece of paper as a trial run. Allow the paper to dry completely, anywhere from 45 minutes to 2 hours, depending on the humidity.

2. Cut the ½ yard of satin into as many 4½" x 8½" pieces as you can get. You should be able to cut at least 16.

3. Protect your ironing board with a couple of layers of scrap fabric or a Teflon pressing sheet, and place a piece of satin on top, right side up. Lay the dry painted paper, dye side down, on the satin. With a hot iron, press down firmly on the paper and keep the iron moving with slow, steady pressure. Don't let the paper shift, or your transfer will blur. Lift one corner of the paper to check if the dye has transferred or if you need to press a bit longer. Set the iron aside; allow the paper to cool slightly, and then lift it off the satin.

4. When the transfer is complete, you will see the dramatic transformation. Evaluate your trial piece and decide whether you want to adjust the strength of the dyes for your remaining paintings. Add a few drops of dye to make it stronger and stir well with the paintbrush. If the color is too strong, add a small amount of water to dilute the mixture.

5. Paint the remaining papers as sky and water and set them aside to dry. It is especially effective to paint more dye on top of your dry paintings to get layers of transparent colors. Iron each one onto the satin pieces. When you have transferred all your paintings to satin, select the sky and water pieces you want for this project and save the rest for other projects. View the satin through the paper frame to help select the most interesting pieces. Cut the sky to 2½" x 7". Iron fusible web to the wrong side

of the water for piece 5 and trim it to 1" x 5½" with a rotary cutter. You are now ready to start composing the landscape.

## MAKING THE LANDSCAPE

Refer to "Pattern and Construction Methods" on page 13 and "The Basic Landscape" on page 15 for instructions as needed.

1. Make a paper frame with an opening of 6" x 7½". Trace two copies of the pattern on page 53 onto tracing paper, one for the placement guide and one for the template pattern.

2. Lay the satin sky across the muslin base. Cut away the background sky piece 1 from the template pattern.

3. Landform pieces 2, 3, and 4 and water piece 5 will all be fused into place. For piece 2, cut the spotted batik to 1½" x 5½"; for piece 3, cut a batik fabric to 1¾" x 5"; and for piece 4, cut a batik fabric to 1¼" x 4¼". Iron fusible web to the wrong side of each piece. They are now ready to be cut into landforms.

4. Lay the template pattern on the right side of the spotted batik for shape 2 and mark the top cutting line. Cut out and place the piece onto the sky. Cut away shape 2 from the template pattern and then repeat the steps for marking and cutting for shapes 3 and 4. Lay the water strip in place covering the bottom of pieces 2, 3, and 4 and flush with the right-hand side. Use the placement guide to adjust the position of the shapes. Make sure that the straight water line is parallel to the top edge of the frame line marked on the placement guide. With a warm iron, lightly fuse these pieces into place so they won't shift while you compose the rest of the landscape.

5. Landform pieces 6, 7, and 8 will be appliquéd by hand. Trim away water piece 5 from the template pattern and mark the top cutting edge of piece 6 onto the batik fabric. Cut it out and place in the composition. Repeat for pieces 7 and 8.

6. Lay the placement guide on the landscape and check the position of all the pieces. Set the placement guide aside, remove pieces 6, 7, and 8, and fuse pieces 2, 3, 4, and 5 permanently in place with a medium-hot iron. Use a clean Teflon pressing sheet, or a cotton pressing cloth to protect the satin from scorching. Don't press too heavily with the iron or the fused landforms under the water may show as a ridge through the satin. Use just enough pressure to fuse them securely. Pin the remaining pieces to be hand appliquéd, and complete the stitching before commencing the next step.

7. In the foreground of this landscape I layered tulle and organza cut in rough tree shapes to echo the impressionistic trees in the fabric for shape 8. Cut a single overlaying piece of tulle to cover the tree shapes and hold them in place. I added simple running stitches to anchor the sheer fabrics. Cut tulle and organza pieces to complement your chosen fabric and add texture and depth to the foreground. For more ideas, check the tulle Design Idea on page 47.

8. Choose a mat frame and mount the landscape, referring to "Mounting and Framing" on page 31.

*Design Ideas*

Once you start using transfer dyes, lots of new possibilities open up. Here are a few suggestions:

- Iron the heat-set transfer dyes onto white synthetic fabrics with a jacquard weave to get interesting textures for skies.

- Organza is wonderfully effective when used with transfer dyes. Paint flower or leaf shapes onto paper with transfer dyes, and then iron the design onto organza. The dyed organza makes transparent overlays on other fabrics and would be perfect to use in "Spring Meadow" on page 70.

- Paint transfer dyes onto leaves. Let them dry; then iron the leaf transfers onto fabric.

*Technique Tip*

When ironing transfers, I use a Teflon pressing sheet both under and on top of the fabric and transfer paper. The sheet protects the ironing board and, when I press hard, the iron glides easily on the Teflon and the paper doesn't shift on the fabric. This eliminates blurred transfers.

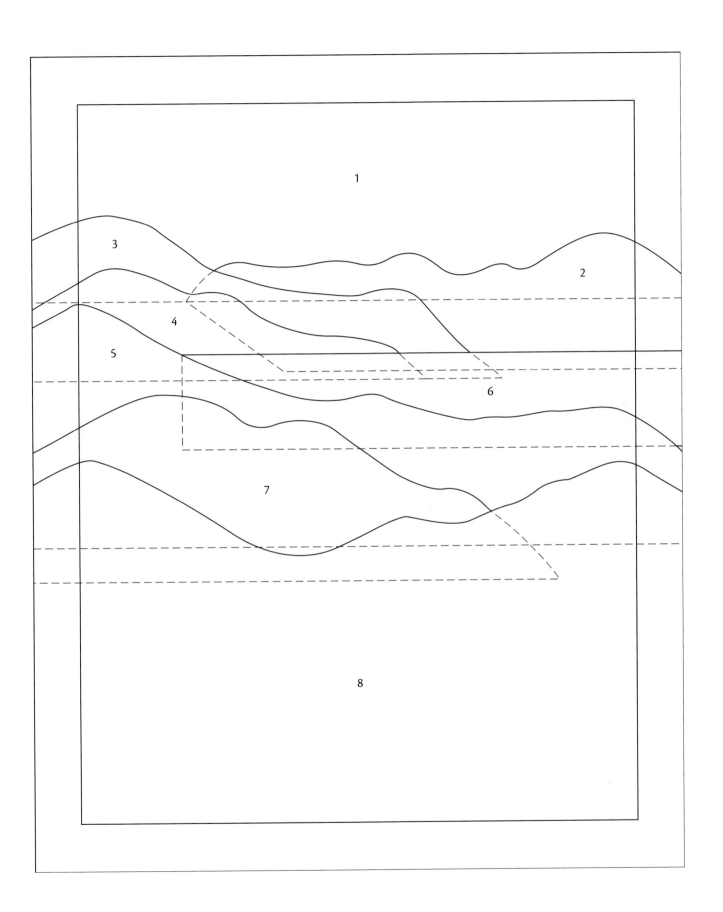

# SHADOWLAND

BY VALERIE HEARDER, 9¼" X 13¼"

**There is something charmingly simple** and direct about coloring with crayons. In this wall hanging I ironed a fabric-crayon transfer onto satin to create the glowing sunset. I used a "highlighting" technique with fabric to outline some of the hills and bring light contrast into the dusky shadows of the landforms. Fusible appliqué makes this a quick project.

**FEATURED TECHNIQUE: CRAYON TRANSFER**

## MATERIALS

*Yardages are based on 42"-wide fabric. All scrap sizes are approximate.*

- ¼ yard of indigo print for outer border
- Fabric scraps:

1 piece, 3" x 6", *each* of green, blue, and purple batiks for hills (3, 4, 5)

1 piece, 6" x 7", of blue batik for foreground

1 piece, 2" x 4", *each* of hot pink for sun and mottled orange/yellow for clouds

1 piece, 4" x 6", of light lavender for highlighting

- 3¾" x 7" piece of satin for sky
- 3" x 7" piece of gold stripe for inner border (A)
- 3¾" x 7" piece of lightweight iron-on stabilizer, such as dressmaker's interfacing
- 10½" x 14¾" piece of fabric for backing
- ¼ yard of fabric for binding
- 10½" x 14¾" piece of cotton batting
- Basic supplies (page 15)
- 4" x 8" piece of white paper
- Fabric crayons
- Teflon pressing sheet
- 8" x 10" piece of fusible web

## PREPARING THE SKY FABRIC

1. Draw a 3¼" x 6" rectangle on the piece of paper. Lay the paper on a smooth surface and color a sunset with fabric crayons in shades of purple, magenta, orange, and yellow. Make a thick layer of color—any spot of white paper will show in your sky.

2. Stabilize the satin by ironing the interfacing to the wrong side, following the manufacturer's instructions. This will be helpful later when you add the inner borders by machine.

3. Protect your ironing board with a double layer of fabric or a Teflon sheet. Lay the satin right side up on the protective fabric and place the crayon transfer face down

on the satin. Press with a hot iron, holding the paper so it doesn't shift. Keep the iron moving, slow and steady, to evenly melt the crayon, but being careful not to melt the satin. Carefully lift a corner of the paper to make sure the crayon has melted onto the satin. It will be obvious when the crayon has stopped melting. Then simply remove the paper from the satin.

4.  Trim the sky piece to 3" x 5¾" after it cools.

## MAKING THE LANDSCAPE

Refer to "Pattern and Construction Methods" on page 13 and "The Basic Landscape" on page 15 for instructions as needed.

1.  Trace two copies of the pattern on page 59 onto tracing paper, one for the placement guide and one for the template pattern.

2.  Embellish the sky piece with fusible appliqué. Begin with the sun; cut a 1" square of hot-pink fabric and iron a 1" square of fusible web to the wrong side using a Teflon pressing sheet. Mark a ¾"-diameter circle on the wrong side and cut it out. Place the sun in the center of the sky, but don't fuse it into place yet. When positioning the circle, allow space for the land-form shape 2 that will cover the bottom edge of the sun.

3.  Iron fusible web to the wrong side of a 2" x 4" piece of mottled, orangish yellow fabric. Cut out curving slivers of wispy cloud shapes and place them onto the sky. When you are satisfied, lightly fuse the shapes into place on the satin sky with a warm iron. This will prevent the small shapes from shifting when you place the Teflon sheet over the composition. Cover the sky with the Teflon sheet and fuse all the shapes permanently into place with a medium-hot iron. Take care; if the temperature is too hot it can melt the satin.

4.  Cut away shapes 1 and 2 from the template pattern. To reduce the buildup of fused layers, use a narrow strip of fusible web across the top edge of each shape. Cut five 1" x 6" pieces of fusible web and one 1" x 6½" piece. For shape 3, cut a 2" x 6" rectangle of green fabric and fuse one of the 6" pieces of web to the top edge, on the wrong side. Using the template pattern, mark the top cutting line of shape 3. Cut it out and place it across the bottom of the sky.

5. Shapes 4 and 5 are outlined with pale lavender, which is what I call a "highlighting" technique. For shape 4, cut a 2¼" x 6" piece of blue fabric and a 1½" x 6" piece of light lavender fabric. Iron a 6" strip of fusible web across the top edge of the wrong side of each piece. Lay the blue fabric on top of the lavender fabric and match up the edges. These pieces will be cut as one unit. Cut away shape 3 from the template pattern and mark the top cutting line on the purple fabric. Pick up the unit and cut out shape 4, cutting through both fabrics at the same time to get an identical cutting line. Slide the top fabric down slightly to expose a ⅛" strip of the lavender—this is the highlight—and place the unit on the green fabric. Use the placement guide to check for accuracy.

*Mark the cutting line on dark fabric; the pale highlight fabric is behind it. Cut the two fabrics as one piece.*

6. Repeat step 5 to cut piece 5 and create a highlight strip. Cut a 2¼" x 6" piece of purple fabric for piece 5 and a 1½" x 6" piece of light lavender fabric for the highlight. Iron a 1" x 6" strip of fusible web across the top edge of the wrong side of each piece. Cut away shape 4 from the template pattern and mark the cutting line for piece 5 on the purple fabric. Layer the two fabrics as you did in step 5 and cut them out together, with the pale lavender strip underneath. Shift the top piece down by ⅛" and place the pieces in the composition. Lay

the placement guide on the unit and line up all the pieces accurately. Then, place the unit on a Teflon sheet and fuse the landforms in place with a medium-hot iron. Don't melt your satin sunset! Lay this unit on a cutting mat and use a rotary cutter to trim the unit to 5¾" wide x 6" tall.

7. From the inner-border fabric (A), cut two strips, ¾" x 6", and one strip, ¾" x 6¼". Using a ¼" seam allowance, machine stitch the shorter 6" strips to the sides of the landscape and then add the top border. Press the seams open. The unit should measure 6¼" x 6¼". Trim and square up the edges if necessary using a rotary cutter and ruler.

8. To add landform piece 6, cut the foreground fabric to 5" x 6½". Iron a 1" x 6½" strip of fusible web across the top on the wrong side. Cut away shape 5 from the template pattern and mark the cutting line for piece 6 on the fabric. Cut it out and position it across the bottom of the landscape, using the placement guide. Fuse in place with a hot iron. Place the whole unit on the cutting mat and, using a ruler and rotary cutter, trim up the edges of shape 6 so they are flush with the edges of the inner borders. Trim the bottom of the unit so that it measures 6¼" wide x 9¾" tall. Measure twice and cut once.

9. From the indigo print, cut two strips, 2" x 14", and one strip, 2" x 13", for the side and top outer borders. These are cut long enough so that the two top corners can be mitered. Refer to "Mitered Borders" on page 34. With a ¼" seam allowance, machine stitch a strip on each side, lining up the strip with the bottom edge so the additional length is at the top of the landscape where the mitered corners will be made. Press the borders open. Then stitch the top border in place, miter the corners, and press the seams open. Cut a 2½" x 9¼" indigo strip for the bottom border and sew it to the quilt.

10. Prepare a quilt sandwich with the backing, batting, and top. Pin the layers together and add machine-quilting lines to the bottom half of piece 6, quilting in the ditch if desired. As an extra highlight, I added a narrow row of machine satin stitching to the indigo borders, using magenta rayon thread to match the color of the sun.

11. When the quilting is complete, trim away the excess backing and batting with a rotary cutter and bind the quilt, referring to "Binding" on page 36.

## Design Ideas

- Add layers of tulle to further embellish the sky. Machine stitch the tulle in place with metallic thread using free-motion embroidery.

- The highlighting technique can be used in any of the projects in this book. It is a great way to inject additional color or contrast in a composition.

## Technique Tip

When creating transfer designs with fabric crayons, lift off any loose flecks of crayon from the paper with a piece of masking tape. This will prevent the flecks from turning into dark spots on the fabric when the iron melts them.

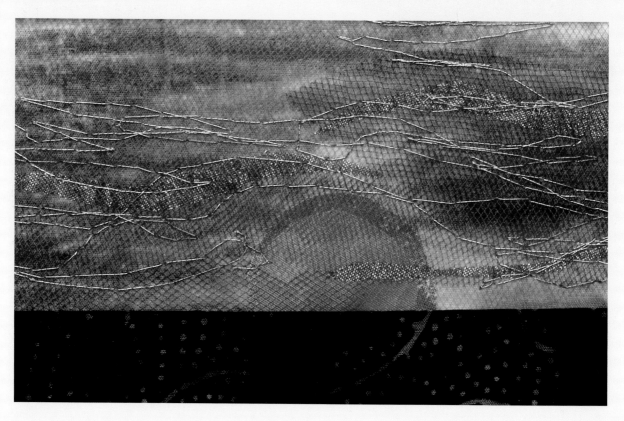

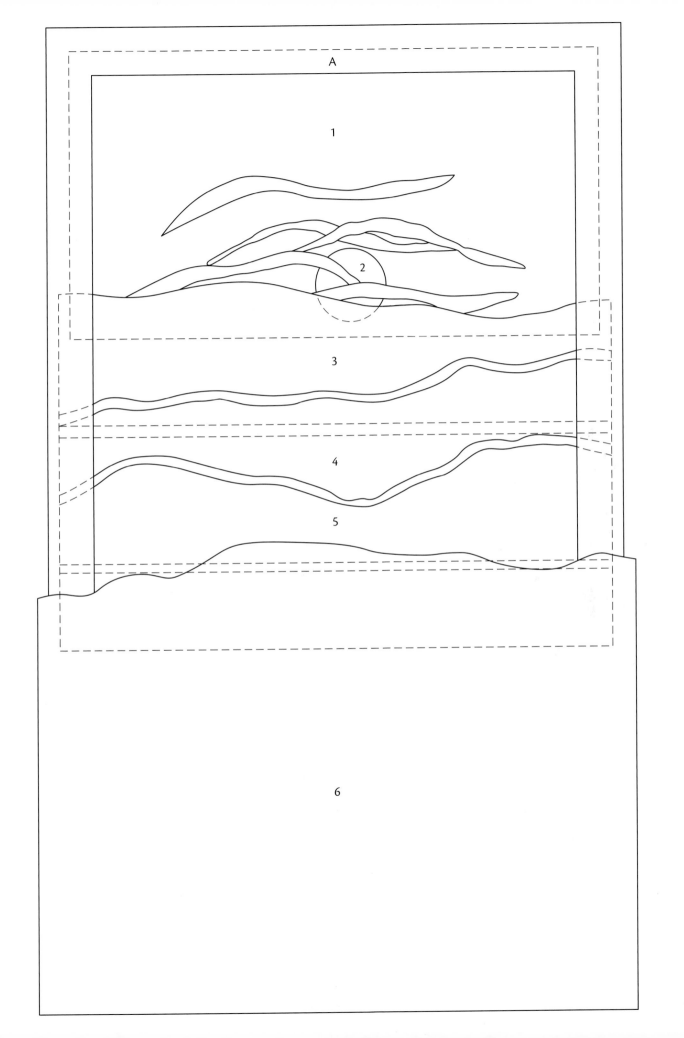

# SOLAR FLARE

BY VALERIE HEARDER, 8¼" X 10½"

**Using oil paint sticks** is rather like coloring with lipstick! It creates thick, creamy color that will cover even dark fabric. In this landscape you'll use a freezer-paper stencil and gold paint stick to color this stylized sun. The bold colors and unusual fabrics—silk and metallic printed cotton—invite you to try out some exciting fabric choices of your own for this landscape. The landforms are all fused, making this a quick and easy project. If you can't locate a paint stick, I've described an alternative using gold metallic fabric (page 62).

FEATURED TECHNIQUE: PAINT STICK

## MATERIALS

*Yardages are based on 42"-wide fabric. All scrap sizes are approximate.*

- Fabric scraps:

  1 piece, 5" x 6", of bright pink for sky

  1 piece, 3" x 3", of orange for sun

  1 piece, 3" x 6", *each* of red and purple for hills

  1 piece, 6" x 8", of green for foreground (silk if desired)

- 1 piece, 6" x 12", of leaf print for inner border (A)

- 1 piece, 6" x 12", of gold stripe for middle border (B)

- 1 piece, 8" x 18", of dark green stripe for outer border (C, D)

- 9½" x 12" piece of fabric for backing

- ⅛ yard of green silk or cotton for binding

- 9" x 11½" piece of cotton batting

- Basic supplies (page 15)

- Freezer paper

- Gold paint stick such as Shiva

- Teflon pressing sheet

- ¼ yard of fusible web

## MAKING THE LANDSCAPE

Refer to "Pattern and Construction Methods" on page 13 and "The Basic Landscape" on page 15 for instructions as needed.

1. Cut a 3¾" x 5¼" piece of pink sky fabric and freezer paper.

2. Make a stencil for the sun by tracing the sun-flare portion of the pattern on page 64 onto freezer paper. The easiest way to do this is to photocopy the pattern and tape it to a light-filled window. Then tape the freezer paper, shiny side down, over the pattern and trace it.

3. Cut away shapes 2 and 3 from the freezer-paper pattern with small scissors and set aside. (You will use shape 3 later.) Lay shape 1 shiny side down onto the sky fabric, lining up the outside edges, and carefully iron the freezer paper with a medium-hot iron so it sticks to the sky fabric. Make sure the inner edge of the freezer paper, with the outline of the sun flare, is adhered well to the fabric. The exposed fabric will be filled in with the paint stick.

4. Prepare the paint stick by using a craft knife to carefully remove the seal that forms over the tip. Be sure to clean up and discard any little flecks that are scraped off—they will create permanent marks.

5. Cover your work surface with scrap paper and lay the fabric with its stencil on the paper. Rub a thick layer of gold paint to completely fill in the exposed fabric. Use care when working the paint into the points of the sun shape so the edge of the stencil doesn't lift. You want a clear line once the stencil is removed.

### Alternative Sun

If you can't locate a paint stick, here is a method to create a similar sun flare using fabric. Iron fusible web to the wrong side of a 4" x 6" piece of gold metallic fabric. Follow the directions in step 1 for tracing a copy of the stencil pattern onto freezer paper. Cut away shape 1 from the freezer paper and discard. Using a Teflon sheet, iron the sun flare (shapes 2 and 3) onto the right side of the fused fabric. With small, sharp scissors, cut out the sun flare closely following the edge of the freezer-paper template. Peel off the freezer paper and fuse the metallic sun onto the sky fabric.

6. Set the gold sun flare aside and allow to dry for 24 to 36 hours, or until no paint comes off to a light touch. There's a slight odor as the volatile oils evaporate, but once it's dry the odor disappears and the color is permanent. To speed up the drying, you can iron the paint stick after about six hours. Protect your ironing board with fabric and cover the painted area with a Teflon sheet or pressing cloth.

7. To make the circle for the center of the sun, cut a 2½" x 2½" piece of orange fabric and iron fusible web onto the wrong side. Cut shape 3 from the freezer-paper pattern that you set aside in step 3. Discard shape 2.

8. Lay the fused orange fabric on the Teflon sheet, and iron freezer-paper shape 3 onto the fabric. Cut the orange circle carefully around the edge of shape 3, remove the paper backing from the fusible web (if it has a backing), and peel off the freezer paper.

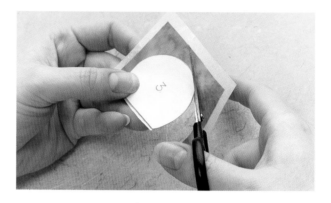

### Gentle Reminder

Don't forget the golden rule: clean the Teflon sheet every time you use it.

9. Position the orange circle on the gold paint-stick sun as indicated on the stencil pattern. If the gold paint isn't completely dry it may transfer to your iron, so cover this sun-and-sky unit with a Teflon sheet and fuse the orange circle into place.

10. Trace two copies of landform shapes 4, 5, and 6 from the pattern on page 65 onto tracing paper. One copy is the template pattern and the other is the placement guide.

11. Cut a 1½" x 5¼" strip of red fabric for shape 4 and, using the Teflon sheet, add fusible web to the wrong side. Cut away the top edge of landform shape 4 on the template pattern, mark the cutting line on the right side of the red fabric, and cut it out. Place the sun-and-sky unit on the Teflon sheet; check the positioning of shape

4 using the placement guide, and then iron into place across the bottom. Leave this unit on the Teflon sheet while the next two pieces are fused in place.

12. Cut a 1½" x 5¼" strip of purple fabric for shape 5 and add fusible web to the wrong side. Cut away shape 4 on the template pattern; lay it on the red fabric and mark the top edge of shape 5. Cut shape 5 and place it across the bottom of red shape 4. Be sure the sun-and-sky unit is lying on a Teflon sheet when you fuse the shapes in place to prevent the unit from sticking to the ironing board. Fuse shape 5 into place over shape 4. Put this fused unit on a cutting mat and use a rotary cutter and ruler to square up and trim the unit to 5¼" wide x 4¾" tall. Be precise with your measuring and cutting.

13. From the leaf print, cut two strips, 1" x 9", and one strip, 1" x 10", for border A. Note that the top corners are mitered; refer to "Mitered Borders" on page 34. Using a ¼" seam allowance, sew a 1" x 9" border to each side and sew the longer strip to the top. If mitering seems too tricky, sew the borders with straight-cut corners. Press the border seams open.

14. Use a rotary cutter and ruler to square up the unit to 6¼" wide x 5¼" tall.

15. Cut a piece of green fabric (I used dupioni silk) to 4½" x 6¼". Fuse a 1" x 6¼" strip of fusible web across the top on the wrong side. Cut away shape 5 from the template pattern. Lay the pattern across the top of the green fabric, mark the top of shape 6, and cut it out. Place the unit on the Teflon sheet and check the position of shape 6 with the placement guide. Iron shape 6 into place across the bottom of

landform piece 5 and border A. With the rotary cutter and ruler, trim and square the unit to 6¼" x 9".

*Sun unit trimmed and squared up, ready for the addition of border B*

16. From the gold striped fabric, cut two strips, ¾" x 9", and one strip, ¾" x 6¾", for border B. Sew a 9" strip to each side and the 6¾" strip to the top to make simple butted corners. Press the border seams open.

17. From the dark green stripe, cut two strips, 1¼" x 14", and one strip, 1¼" x 12", for border C. Sew a longer strip to each side and the shorter strip across the top, mitering the corners. Cut a 1½" x 8½" strip from the green stripe and sew it to the bottom to form border piece D (see page 65). Press the border seams open. Trim and square up the edges so the quilt top measures 8¼" x 10½".

18. Mark the quilting lines with an erasable marker such as a chalk liner. Lay the quilt top over the cotton batting and backing and pin in place. Thread your machine with gold metallic thread. Use a large-eyed embroidery machine needle and stitch slowly to avoid breaking the thread. I also quilted approximately ⅛" from the border seams.

19. Bind the quilt using the green silk or cotton, referring to "Binding" on page 36. Add a 1½"-wide hanging sleeve, referring to "Hanging Sleeve" on page 36.

## Design Idea

Now that you know how to make a stencil, you can fill in the design elements with oil pastel, embossing powder, acrylic paint, or other mediums. In this photo, I cut out a stencil of leaf shapes and filled it with gold paint stick. I machine quilted the leaf veins with metallic thread.

## Technique Tip

Silk is a wonderful fabric that's easy to work with when you stabilize it on the wrong side with lightweight iron-on dressmaker's interfacing. The interfacing adds body and prevents fraying.

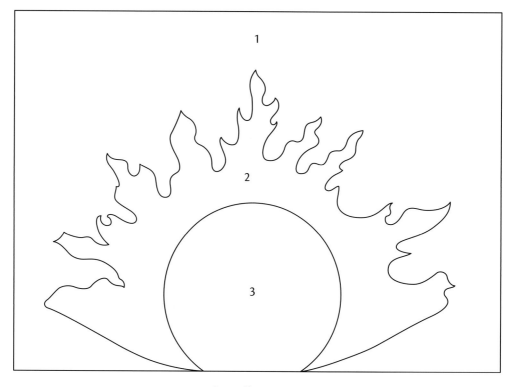

**Stencil pattern**

# SUMMER MARSH

BY VALERIE HEARDER, 7¾" X 5"

It's magical to see a piece of fabric take on new dimension by embellishing it with colored-pencil details. This landscape is simple in its elements, yet the addition of marsh grass using colored pencils and stitching creates texture and movement. I used Ranger Heat Set Inks to paint the sky; however, you can use any fabric paints of your choice or use purchased hand-dyed sky fabric. This landscape is entirely fused.

**FEATURED TECHNIQUE: COLORED PENCILS**

## MATERIALS

*All scrap sizes are approximate.*

- 6" x 8¾" piece of muslin for base
- 3" x 9" piece of satin for sky
- Fabric scraps:

  1 piece, 1" x 1", of orange for sun

  1 piece, 2" x 8", of dark green for hills

  1 piece, 3" x 9", of stripe for water

  1 piece, 4" x 10", *each* of 2 greens for grass

- Threads for embellishing
- Basic supplies (page 15)
- Teflon pressing sheet
- ¼ yard of fusible web
- Colored pencils in shades of green
- Mat frame

## MAKING THE LANDSCAPE

Refer to "Pattern and Construction Methods" on page 13 and "The Basic Landscape" on page 15 for instructions as needed. Also be sure to read "Fusible Appliqué" on page 22.

1. Trace two copies of the pattern on page 69 onto tracing paper, one for the placement guide and one for the template pattern. Make a paper frame with an opening of 5" x 7¾".

2. If you are using Ranger Heat Set Inks to make an iron-on transfer for the sky, follow the directions on page 24. I used blue, yellow, and red for this sky. Trim the satin or sky fabric to 2¾" x 8½". Place the sky on the muslin base.

3. Iron fusible web to the wrong side of the 1" x 1" square of orange fabric (I used silk). Draw a ⅝"-diameter circle onto the fused side and cut it out for the sun—the base of a thimble should be about the right size. Lay it on the sky, but don't fuse it in place yet.

4. Cut away pieces 1 and 2 from the template pattern. For landform shape 3, cut a 1½" x 7¼" piece of dark green fabric and iron fusible web to the wrong side. Lay the template pattern onto the right side of the fabric and trace the top edge of shape 3. Cut it out and place it on the sky.

5. For water piece 4, I used a striped fabric with a fine grassy-looking print. The stripes add a sense of depth. Choose a suitable fabric for the water and cut it to 2¼" x 8½". Iron a 1" strip of fusible web to the top edge on the wrong side. Trim the top edge with a rotary cutter to get a straight water horizon line. Lay the water piece across the bottom edge of shape 3 and use the placement guide to position the sun and the landform piece. Fuse pieces 2, 3, and 4 into place with a dry, medium-hot iron and a Teflon sheet to protect the satin from melting.

6. For marsh pieces 5 and 6, I used a commercial fabric in a mottled batik with light areas that allow the colored pencil marks to show up well. For piece 5, cut one of the green fabrics to 3" x 8½". Iron a 1" strip of fusible

web to the top edge on the wrong side. Cut away shape 4 from the template pattern; lay the pattern on the right side of the fabric and mark the cutting line for piece 5. Cut it out and place it over the water using the placement guide to check positioning. Repeat for shape 6 using the second green fabric. Once you are satisfied with the position of all the pieces, fuse shapes 5 and 6 into place using a dry, medium-hot iron and a pressing sheet.

7. To draw the marsh grass with colored pencils, place the landscape on a hard surface. Choose colored pencils in three different shades of green, from dark to light—be sure to include a nice, bright lime green. Sharpen the colored pencils so you can make crisp marks. You may want to practice on a scrap of fabric first to play around with making grassy marks. Hold the landscape in place and draw firmly to make strong, bold grassy strokes. Draw plenty of marks, as they will be covered with stitches and you want the marks to be visible. When you have finished drawing, pin the landscape to the muslin base to create additional support for the stitches.

8. Thread a needle with a single strand of green thread. I used four different green threads—dark, medium, light, and lime green—which added a lively highlight. Rayon has a nice shine, but ordinary machine or embroidery thread is also effective. Make simple, random straight stitches—some short and some long—following your pencil marks as a guide. Refer to the photo above right and to the illustration of the straight stitch in "Stitchery" on page 28. Remember to pause every now and then to review how the stitches are flowing across the

grass—you want the stitches to look like grass moving in the breeze. When you are done stitching, finish off on the wrong side of the landscape with a few backstitches.

9. Press the landscape and pin the paper frame to it. Choose a custom-cut mat frame and mount your landscape referring to "Mounting and Framing" on page 31.

### Design Idea

Oil pastels are another option for drawing directly on fabric. They look like short, fat crayons without a point, and they give a softer look than pencils. Here I used regular school-grade oil pastels and blended the colors with my finger before they dried. Embellishment with simple embroidery stitches and a few beads adds further rich texture.

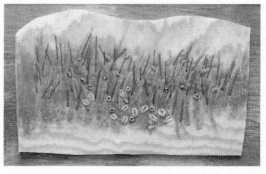

### Technique Tips

Look at the hand-dyed fabric used for the green hill (shape 3). A colored pencil could easily achieve the effect of the darker hill contours. When I want to create some water fabric quickly, I use water-based colored pencils to draw on fabric and then add water to dissolve the pencil marks.

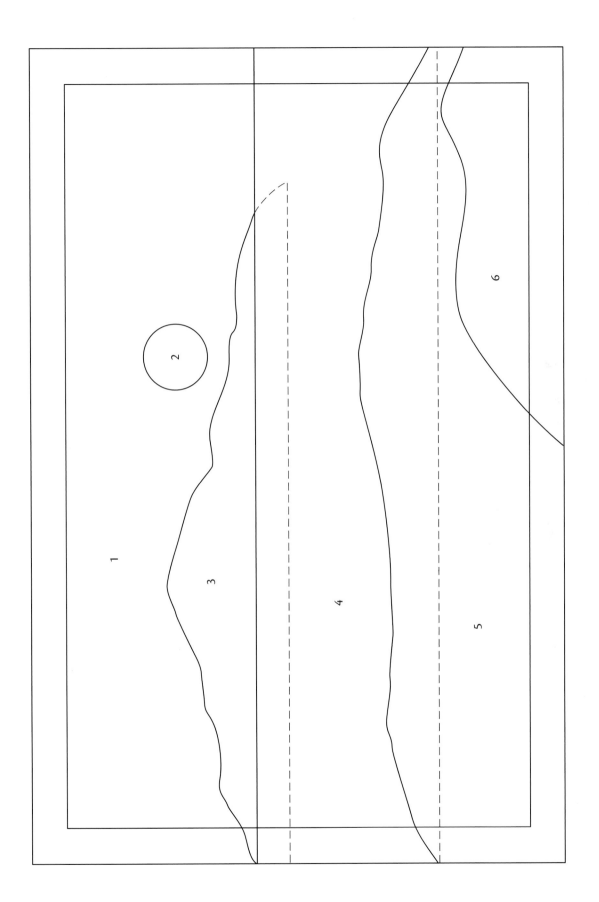

SUMMER MARSH

# SPRING MEADOW

BY VALERIE HEARDER, 6¼" X 9"

**In this project a delicate spring** meadow blossoms with beads and stitches over printed tulle. The tulle lets the grassy fabric show through, creating depth. Layer scraps of netting, organza, and colored lace, and anchor them with these simple embroidery stitches and beads to create added texture and movement in this delightful composition. You could also make your own grassy meadow fabric with colored pencils as shown in "Summer Marsh" on page 66. This landscape is mostly hand appliquéd, with fusible appliqué details for the sun and water.

### FEATURED TECHNIQUES: BEADING, EMBROIDERY

## MATERIALS

*All scrap sizes are approximate.*

- 7¼" x 10" piece of muslin for base
- Fabric scraps:

  1 piece, 4" x 8", of fabric for sky (1)

  1 piece, 1" x 1", of orange for sun (2)

  1 piece, 3" x 9", *each* of pink and lavender for hills (3, 4)

  1 piece, 3" x 8", of blue for water (5)

  1 piece, 4" x 8", *each* of bright green, pink, and blue for hills (6, 7, 8)

  1 piece, 6" x 8", of green for foreground (9)

- 3" x 9" piece of pink tulle
- Scraps of tulle, organza, or netting, 5" x 9"
- Basic supplies (page 15)
- Teflon pressing sheet
- 4" x 8" piece of fusible web
- Embroidery threads and beads
- Mat frame

## MAKING THE LANDSCAPE

Refer to "Pattern and Construction Methods" on page 13 and "The Basic Landscape" on page 15 for instructions as needed.

1. Trace two copies of the pattern on page 74 onto tracing paper, one for the placement guide and one for the template pattern. Make a paper frame with an opening of 6¼" x 9".

2. Cut the sky fabric to 3" x 7¼" and lay it on the muslin base. Prepare a sun shape by ironing fusible web to the wrong side of the 1" x 1" square of orange fabric. Draw a circle on the wrong side using the pattern for piece 2. Cut it out and set aside.

3. Cut away pieces 1 and 2 from the template pattern and mark the top edge of piece 3 onto the pink fabric. Cut it out and place it on the sky. Trim away piece 3 from the template pattern and mark the top cutting edge of piece 4 on the lavender fabric. Cut it out and place it in the landscape. Use the placement guide to position the pieces accurately, and then pin them securely and hand appliqué in place.

4. When pieces 3 and 4 are stitched in place, press them to lie flat. Cut a 1¼" x 5⅜" strip of blue fabric for water piece 5. (I made the water fabric using transfer dyes on satin as discussed on page 24.) Iron fusible web

to the wrong side of the water fabric using a Teflon pressing sheet. Trim the top edge with a rotary cutter to get a straight water horizon line, and place it across the bottom of piece 4. Check the positioning with the placement guide. Lay the paper frame on the landscape to make sure the water horizon is parallel to the top edge of the pattern; iron it into place with a pressing cloth to protect any delicate fabrics. Position the sun on the sky and iron it in place.

5. Trim piece 5 from the template pattern and mark the top edge of piece 6 onto bright green fabric, including the dotted extension lines. Cut it out and place it over the water piece. Repeat for pieces 7, 8, and 9. Use the placement guide to adjust the pieces and then pin them in place. Hand appliqué pieces 6, 7, and 8. Leave the edge of piece 9 raw and attach it to piece 8 using straight, vertical embroidery stitches.

6. Before adding embroidery, cut pieces of colored tulle, organza, colored lace, netting, or sheer fabrics. Arrange them in a collage of leaf shapes across the bottom of piece 9. When the pieces are arranged, iron them with a warm iron, pin them in place, and embellish with straight stitches for grass. Add French knots and beads to create an impression of flowers. I used both double and single strands of embroidery floss for the straight stitches. Vary the scale of the stitches and create a sense of depth by making the stitches larger at the bottom of the foreground piece and smaller near the top. See "Stitchery" on page 28.

7. Cut two or three pieces of pink tulle into cloud shapes large enough that the edges extend to the top and side of the sky fabric. Use a running stitch to attach the tulle close to the edge as shown. The mat frame will cover the stitches and the tulle will be protected from snags after framing.

8. Choose a mat frame with an opening of 6¼" x 9". I chose a custom-cut mat with a curved top in the Palladian style, but a simple rectangular opening would work just as well. See "Mounting and Framing" on page 31.

SPRING MEADOW

## Design Ideas

A quick and easy way to add interesting texture to a landscape is to fray the edge of a landform instead of turning it under. It's a bit easier to fray a piece that is cut fairly straight or with a gentle curve. Fray the edges and cut the fringe at different lengths. Use simple running stitches or other straight embroidery stitches to attach the raw edge to the background.

Stretch tulle is a mesh fabric, a bit heavier than regular tulle with some spandex in it. It's often used in skating costumes and lingerie. Buy plain white stretch tulle and color it using iron-on transfer dyes such as Ranger Heat Set Inks. (Refer to "Iron-on Transfer Dyes" on page 24.) Mix a small amount of the transfer dyes in flowery colors. Make the dyes strong and add only enough water to allow the dyes to be painted onto a sheet of paper. Use a simple approach—no need for fine details, just make blobs of dye in flower shapes. Paint the background around the flowers with dye so no white paper shows. When the painting is dry, place the netting, or other sheer fabric such as organza, on a Teflon sheet. Place the dry painting over it, cover it with another layer of Teflon, and iron it with a medium-hot iron. Watch the heat carefully, as the sheer fabrics are delicate and can melt easily. Another option is to paint directly on the netting with diluted acrylic paints.

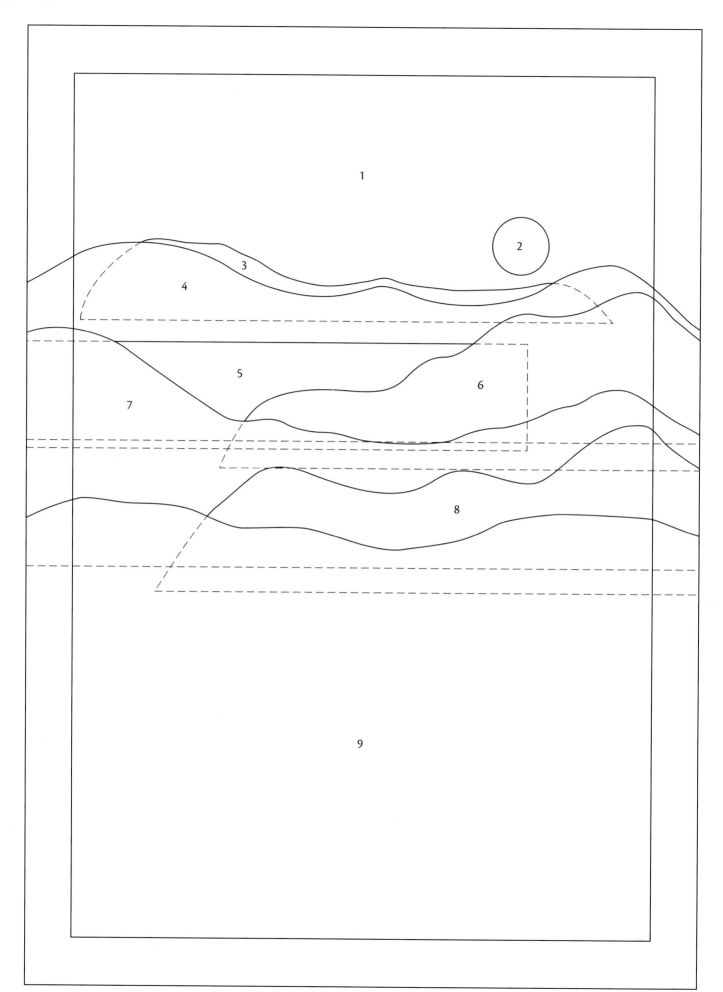

SPRING MEADOW

# FERN HILL

BY VALERIE HEARDER, 6½" X 7½"

**My collection of South African** sun-print fabrics is an endless source of inspiration. They are dyed on the banks of a river in Africa with indigenous leaves and have an impressionistic look. Happily, these fabrics are now more readily available. I used a vanishing muslin stabilizer to add a heavily free-motion stitched fringe to the foreground hill. This loosely woven stabilizer provides a stiff base that can sustain dense machine stitching. When ironed, the vanishing muslin base disintegrates, leaving only the stitches. You can stitch elements such as leaves, trees, fences, or even a scarecrow to add a special focus in your landscape.

**FEATURED TECHNIQUES: VANISHING MUSLIN, MACHINE EMBROIDERY**

## MATERIALS

*All scrap sizes are approximate.*

- 7½" x 8½" piece of muslin for base
- Fabric scraps:

   1 piece, 4" x 8", of pale blue for sky (1)

   1 piece, 4" x 8", of green for hill (2)

   1 piece, 3" x 8", of pink for hill (3)

   1 piece, 3" x 8", of pale blue for water (4)

   1 piece, 4" x 8", each of pale peach and pink-and-peach for hills (5, 6)

   1 piece, 4" x 8", of mottled green for foreground (7)

   Leaf prints for foreground

- Basic supplies (page 15)
- 4" x 8½" piece of vanishing muslin (Sulky Heat-Away)
- Mat frame

## MAKING THE LANDSCAPE

Refer to "Pattern and Construction Methods" on page 13 and "The Basic Landscape" on page 15 for instructions as needed.

1. Trace two copies of the pattern on page 79 onto tracing paper, one for the placement guide and one for the template pattern. Make a paper frame with an opening of 6½" x 7½".

2. Cut the sky fabric to 3" x 7½" and lay it on the muslin base. Trim away sky piece 1 from the pattern. Mark the top cutting edge of piece 2 onto the green fabric. Cut it out and place it in the landscape composition. Repeat this step using the pink fabric for piece 3.

3. For the water (piece 4), cut out a 1½" x 7½" rectangle and place it in the landscape. Trim away pieces 3 and 4 from the template pattern, and mark the top cutting edge for piece 5 on the pale peach fabric. Cut it out and place it in the composition. Repeat this step for piece 6 using the pink-and-peach fabric. When

piece 6 is positioned, use the placement guide to adjust all the pieces so they are accurately placed; pay particular attention to the water horizon. Lay the paper frame over the piece to make sure the water line is parallel to the top edge of the frame. Pin all the pieces thoroughly and, starting with green piece 2, hand appliqué each piece in sequence until piece 6 is stitched in place.

4. Trim away piece 6 from the template pattern and mark the cutting line for piece 7 on the mottled green fabric. Cut it out. The top edge of this piece will be embellished with machine stitches using the vanishing muslin.

5. Fold the 4" x 8½" piece of vanishing muslin in half. Place piece 7 on the vanishing muslin so that about 1" of the muslin extends above the top of piece 7. Hand baste piece 7 to the vanishing muslin. Before you begin the free-motion stitching, I suggest you read through steps 6, 7, and 8; make a practice piece to get the rhythm of the stitching. Refer to "Machine Embroidery" on page 29.

6. Choose thread colors to complement your landscape fabrics. I used four different colors—lavender, light green, medium green, and pink—to make the textured fringe. Variegated thread is a perfect choice because it adds a nice blend of colors; I also like to use rayon thread for its luster. Thread the top of the machine with lavender thread and the bobbin with pale green.

7. Place piece 7 layered with the vanishing muslin under the needle and lower the darning foot. While the machine is running quite fast, move the muslin gently back and forth in a steady motion under the needle to make rows of stitches. Catch about ½" of piece 7 and extend the stitching past the edge of piece 7 into the vanishing muslin by about ½". This will create

the fringe when the muslin is removed. Vary the length of the stitched rows and make them uneven, with some rows long and some short.

8. When you have made one pass over the edge with stitches that are quite close together, thread your machine again with different colors in the top and bobbin. Repeat the process, adding another layer of free-form stitches until the edge of piece 7 and the vanishing muslin extension are densely covered. When you feel you have enough stitches, remove the unit from the sewing machine and trim away the excess muslin, close to the stitches. Also trim the excess muslin from the wrong side of the piece and remove the basting stitches.

9. Place the stitched piece on the ironing board between two layers of Teflon pressing sheet to protect both the ironing board from the stabilizer ash and the stitches from the high heat. Heat a dry iron to its highest temperature and iron for about 30 seconds until you notice the vanishing muslin starting to turn brown and then black as it chars and begins to crumble. Set the iron aside and gently brush away the charred muslin with your fingers or an old toothbrush. Repeat the ironing process until

the muslin has disintegrated on the front and back. Piece 7 now has a soft fringe of colored threads.

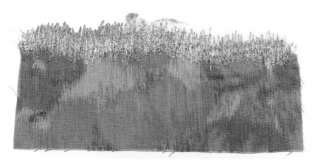

*Here you can see the vanishing muslin has been trimmed away and some of it is charred. The left side shows where the muslin has been disintegrated and removed, leaving just the stitches.*

10. Stitch the bottom edge of piece 7 to the background muslin base. This piece is the foundation on which to compose the leaf collage. To add a greater sense of depth, I left the fringe floating free of the background rather than stitching it down flat.

11. Look for interesting leaf fabrics to make a collage for the foreground. I cut nine separate leaf shapes and ironed fusible web to the wrong side to prevent the edges from fraying. Using a Teflon sheet, iron the leaf shapes to fuse them together into a single unit. To add interest, I machine stitched leaf vein details with a very narrow stitch length. This also served to attach the leaf unit to the foreground. To do this, use a sheet of paper or other foundation material underneath while stitching. Remove the paper after the stitching is complete. Sew the leaf collage to the bottom edge of the landscape by machine. To keep building a sense of depth, leave the rest of the leaf unit floating free. You could simply fuse the leaf unit to the foreground if you prefer. For more information and ideas about making the leaf collage, look over the instructions for the leaf collage in "Late Afternoon View" on pages 41 and 42.

12. Choose a mat frame and mount the landscape, referring to "Mounting and Framing" on page 31.

## Design Idea

To make a fence element for the tiny landscape shown below, I laid a double piece of vanishing muslin over my drawing of a fence and traced it directly onto the muslin. Using free-motion machine embroidery, I filled in the fence with stitches until the drawing was completely filled and the stitches were all crisscrossed. It's important to cross over the stitches to link them together, otherwise, when the vanishing muslin disintegrates, the stitching will come apart. When the stitching is complete and the vanishing muslin has been removed, all that's left is the thread appliqué, ready to be a charming detail in the landscape. I hand stitched the fence into place and then added a few grassy hand stitches around the base of each fence post.

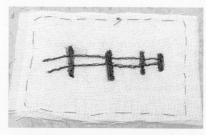

## Technique Tip

You may need to use tweezers to pull out any stray threads of the vanishing muslin that didn't "vanish" with the heat.

FERN HILL

FERN HILL

# AUTUMN OAK

BY VALERIE HEARDER, 7½" X 5½"

I adore leaf shapes, which are such a strong design element, and trees hold special significance for me, so it seemed natural to include a tree pattern among my small landscapes. Here is an opportunity to try out confetti appliqué—or "flash-and-trash," as I call it. It's easy to stitch without a hoop when you use a heavyweight water-soluble stabilizer; simply pin the layers together for free-motion stitching.

## FEATURED TECHNIQUE: CONFETTI APPLIQUÉ

## MATERIALS

*All scrap sizes are approximate.*

- 6½" x 8½" piece of muslin for base
- Fabric scraps:

  1 piece, 6" x 10", of sky fabric (1)

  1 piece, 1½" x 1½", of pale peach for sun (2)

  1 piece, 3" x 10", *each* of 3 lavenders or blues for hills (3, 4, 5)

  1 piece, 3" x 10", of light green for plains (6)

  1 piece, 4" x 10", of leafy batik for foreground (7)

  1 piece, 5" x 5", of brown for tree

  1 piece, 2½" x 2½", *each* of 5 different fabrics for leaves

- 3½" x 5" piece of green organza or other sheer fabric
- ⅜ yard of paper-backed fusible web such as Wonder Under
- 10" x 14" piece of Fabri-Solvy
- Mat frame

## MAKING THE LANDSCAPE

Refer to "Pattern and Construction Methods" on page 13 and "The Basic Landscape" on page 15 for instructions as needed.

1. Trace two copies of the pattern on page 84 onto tracing paper, one for the placement guide and one for the template pattern. Make a paper frame with an opening of 5½" x 7½".

2. Cut the sky fabric to 3¾" x 8½" and lay it on the muslin base. Cut three 1¼" x 6½" strips of lavender or blue fabrics for the distant hill pieces 3, 4, and 5. Cut one 1¼" x 8½" strip of light green fabric for piece 6. Iron fusible web onto the back of each strip.

3. Cut away the sky (including piece 2) from the template pattern and trace the top edge of piece 3 onto one of the distant hill strips. Cut it out and place it on the sky. Repeat for pieces 4, 5, and 6. Use the placement guide to check for accurate positioning of each piece and then fuse pieces 3, 4, 5, and 6 into place in the landscape composition.

### Morning Sun

I chose a subtle color for the sun, close to the color of the sky, to suggest the look of a morning sunrise.

4. To make the sun, place a 1" square of paper-backed fusible web onto the template pattern and trace the circle (piece 2). Iron the fusible web to the pale peach scrap. Cut out the sun, peel off the paper, and fuse it into the landscape.

5. Cut a 4" x 4" piece of paper-backed fusible web. Trace the pattern for the tree trunk and branches on page 85 onto fusible web. Iron the fusible web to the wrong side of the brown fabric and use small scissors to carefully cut out the tree along the traced lines. Peel off the paper backing and fuse your tree into the landscape using the placement guide.

6. For piece 7, cut the leafy batik to 2¾" x 8½". Iron a 1" x 8½" strip of fusible web along the top on the wrong side. Cut away piece 6 from the template pattern and trace the top edge of piece 7 onto the fabric. Cut it out and iron it into place with the help of the placement guide.

7. To make the confetti leaves for the tree, stack the 2½" squares of fabric on a cutting mat. Slice up the fabric finely with a rotary cutter and ruler by first cutting narrow ⅛" strips. Then move the ruler and cut on the diagonal to create diamond shapes. Space each cut no more than ⅛" apart.

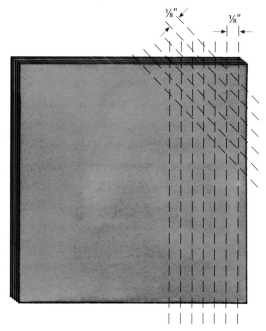

8. Cut two 5" x 7" pieces of Fabri-Solvy and trace the leaf crown outline on page 85 onto both pieces. Turn the pieces over so that the pattern is reversed. Cover one of the tracings with a piece of green organza, and sprinkle the confetti leaves onto the organza. Spread the leaves so they cover the organza in the shape of the tree pattern, but not too thickly, as it's nice to have a lacy effect with small areas of the trunk and background showing through. Cover the confetti with the other piece of Fabri-Solvy so that the tree tracings line up.

9. Pin the three layers together as shown in preparation for free-motion stitching. Note that you can also use a water-soluble stabilizer (such as Solvy) stretched in a hoop to do the stitching. Follow the manufacturer's instructions for using the stabilizer.

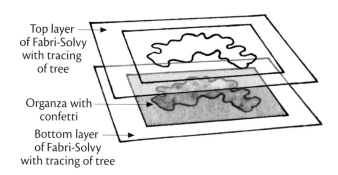

Top layer of Fabri-Solvy with tracing of tree

Organza with confetti

Bottom layer of Fabri-Solvy with tracing of tree

10. Prepare your machine for free-motion stitching by dropping the feed dogs and attaching the darning foot. Thread with a rayon machine thread—I used orange in both the top and the bobbin. First stitch around the traced tree shape and then fill in the shape with a circular, meandering, free-motion pattern to make sure the tree crown shape is covered and most of the confetti is caught by stitches.

11. Remove the pins, trim away all the excess Fabri-Solvy about ½" from the stitched edge, and soak the confetti layers in a bowl of warm water to dissolve the stabilizer. Keep rinsing until the sticky residue is washed out. Press the confetti leaves between two pieces of cloth to dry. Trim away the excess organza underlay and stitch the tree crown into place over the branches by hand.

12. Add the final touches to your landscape by machine stitching in the foreground. I used the leaves of my leafy print as a guide.

13. Choose a mat frame and mount the landscape, referring to "Mounting and Framing" on page 31.

## Design Idea

How about a Red Delicious apple tree instead of an oak? Use green confetti leaves and stitch juicy-looking red beads on by hand. Confetti appliqué also makes lovely foreground foliage in a landscape. Cut up decorative threads and metallic fabric into confetti to make exotic embellishments.

## Technique Tip

You can use a temporary spray adhesive to help baste the layers of Fabri-Solvy together with the organza and confetti. Spray the Fabri-Solvy with an adhesive; then create a sandwich with the confetti and organza. This will help hold the layers together—but I'd recommend adding pins as well. The spray adhesive is temporary but not water soluble, so once stitching is complete, press the sandwich with a warm iron to dissipate the spray glue before soaking the stitchery in warm water.

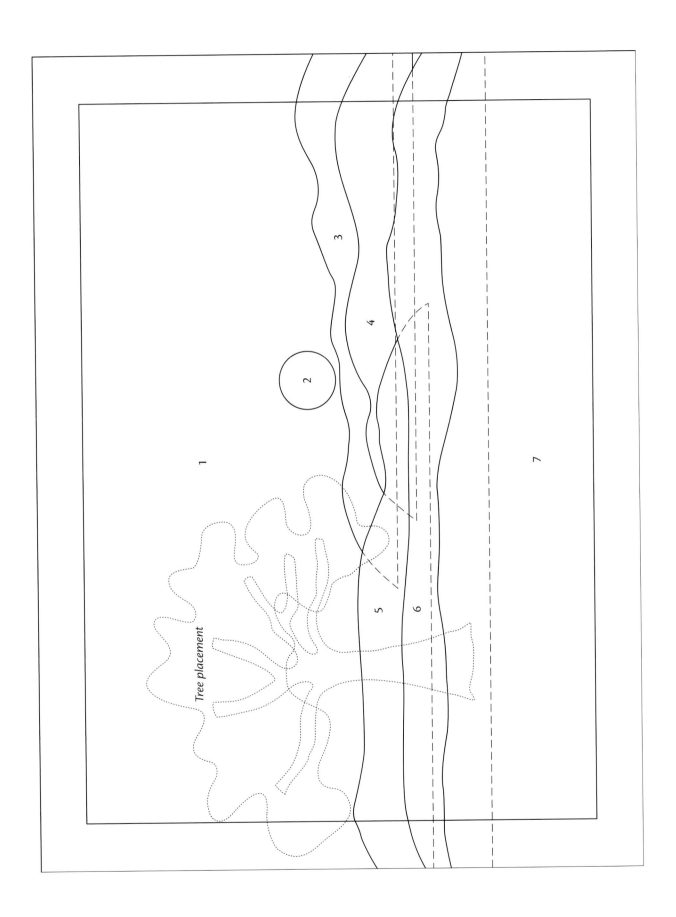

Tree placement

1

2

3

4

5

6

7

AUTUMN OAK

2

1

Pattern is reversed
for fusible-web appliqué.

# DESIGN NOTES

Making fabric landscapes of your own design is an exciting journey. The landscapes we live in, those we hold in our memories, and those that exist only in our imaginations are an unending source of inspiration. Our treasured fabrics and their patterns, colors, and textures are also a wellspring of design possibilities. In this section, I'll encourage you to tap into the inspiration of landscape and the love of textiles to create your own original compositions using my "cut-and-collage" approach to free-form composition of fabric landscapes.

This part of the book is different from the previous parts in that it doesn't provide a pattern for you to follow. There are two reasons for this. First, as you have followed the patterns for earlier projects you will have gained all the technical information you need to make your own patterns for landscape designs. You will have a good grasp of the system or method that I use. Second, and more important, I want to empower you to go beyond my designs and patterns, to discover your own creativity and courage, and to make your own compositions. I will explain the processes and principles of a free-form cut-and-collage process that I use to create my fabric landscapes. These processes and principles form the basis of all the patterns in this book, and they can be summarized as follows:

- Let the fabric lead the design.
- Start with the sky.
- Layer the fabric from the sky to the foreground, working from the top of the landscape to the bottom.
- Use your scissors as your brush or drawing pencil to create the fabric landform shapes, colors, patterns, and textures.
- Experiment, play, and try many fabric options in the composition.

- Trust your eye.
- Use a frame to help your eye to define the composition.
- Step back and view from a distance.

## FABRIC LEADS THE DESIGN

When I make landscapes, I seldom follow a sketch or a photo. My landscapes come from experimenting, taking inspiration from the colors and patterns in the fabrics, and trusting my eye to tell me what works. But it all starts with fabric. I enjoy the process of searching for an interesting, unexpected fabric that suggests a hill, valley, or sunrise. Be sure to read "Fabric: Our Paint Palette" beginning on page 8, where I discuss fabric choices in depth. Fabric is the cornerstone for the spontaneous design of original landscapes.

Try not to be conservative with the amount of fabric you need to cut, as this will restrict the creative flow and possibilities. I may try 15 or even 20 different fabric combinations in my search for the most pleasing landscape composition. I adore cutting and playing with multiple fabric options, and what does a quilter enjoy more? I'm never quite sure what the landscape will look like until it's done. Because the outcome is always new and unpredictable, it's endlessly interesting. It can sometimes be a greater challenge to work with a free-form approach, and there have been times when I have spent an entire day collaging fabrics only to abandon the landscape because the design just didn't gel. The fabric snips may end up in my "scraps-too-small-to-save" box, but the design process is never wasted. Each composition, successful or not, teaches me so much about design. It's this learning curve that is invaluable and the experience can only be gained when you are willing to go beyond working from a pattern and risk mistakes.

## START WITH THE SKY

The sky is the background for the landforms and is the first fabric I choose and lay down on the muslin base. The colors in the sky set the atmosphere and tone of the landscape. Pastels will evoke impressions of gentle summer days while dark, strong colors may suggest a stormy sky. If you are struggling with a design and you have rearranged the landforms repeatedly trying to make it work, try changing the sky fabric. Often we start out with a particular sky choice and, as the landscape evolves, we realize that the sky is no longer effective. Try something lighter, darker, or brighter. The key is to keep trying out different fabrics until you find the fabric that makes the landscape sing.

### Tiny Landscapes from Tiny Scraps

Lyn Barrett-Cowan of Mississauga, Canada, uses fabric scraps that are usually thrown out to make her miniature landscapes on cards. Each landscape is original because it would be impossible to duplicate the size and shape of each fabric. Small fabric snippets are like gold to Lyn. A Russian stitcher, whom Lyn taught, makes similar cards in support of an orphanage. Lyn says, "My idea travels halfway around the world to help children. I really like that."

*Calm by Lyn Barrett-Cowan, 4" x 3" (shown actual size)*

I don't use a template or mark cutting lines; I simply cut out each landform shape freehand. Cut and collage is a synergistic process of cutting fabric free form while trusting my eye to tell me what's working or not. I keep cutting and rearranging the shapes and colors, trying many different options, until I'm satisfied with both the composition and the colors. The key to successful cut and collage is willingness to play with the fabrics and make spontaneous changes to the composition as it develops. The more you are willing to experiment, the more you'll enjoy the spontaneity of the process. Experimenting wastes very little fabric and rejected pieces can always be saved for another landscape project. Experimenting gives you options and teaches design.

As you try different compositions, it's important to view them from a distance. Step back, or look at the piece through a reducing glass or a pair of binoculars turned backward to get distance from the work. You can't make a design decision until the fabric is cut out, placed in the composition, and you have something to evaluate. The key is to develop the landscape by playing with the fabric and making many spontaneous changes to the composition while trusting your innate sense of what works and what does not, ultimately leading you to a design that makes you happy.

## PAPER FRAME

The paper frame is a useful design aid when composing a free-form landscape. It helps define the landscape's proportions and enables you to evaluate the effectiveness of each shape in the composition. Because the free-form landscape is evolving as you make it, and you don't know what the final size will be, make an adjustable viewfinder frame out of two L shapes that you can easily make smaller or bigger as needed—just like we did in "Seeing Fabric with Fresh Eyes" (page 8).

To make a frame, use two sheets of ordinary legal-size paper, 8½" x 14", and cut a 2"-wide L shape from each sheet. Refer to page 8 for an illustration and additional details for making a viewfinder frame. For these purposes, larger paper will make a more versatile frame.

Lay the paper frame over the landscape to evaluate the effect of each new shape that is cut and positioned in the landscape. Adjust the size of the viewfinder opening as the composition develops to see how it will work bigger or smaller, horizontally or vertically.

## FADE INTO THE DISTANCE

When you observe a landscape in real life, it often seems to fade from dark or strong in the foreground to gradually paler layers as you look farther into the distance. This is because of atmospheric haze and this formula makes for a very pleasing landscape. But if you study photographs and paintings you will notice that the placement of light and dark is far more varied, depending on time of day and how the view is cropped. In my experience sometimes a landscape can be light or dark at different viewpoints in the landscape—there is no rigid law that states where darks and light should fall. If every landscape is created based on a progression from dark to light, it could soon become a predictable formula, and I fear they may all start looking too much alike. Besides, my goal is not to make an exact copy of nature, but rather an impressionistic feeling of nature. Experiment with your own choices. You have creative freedom to make what pleases your eye. Be adventurous and trust your own judgment, unhampered by traditional rules.

*Dusk by Valerie Hearder, 4¾" x 5½".
Although landscapes are often darker in the foreground
and lighter as they recede toward the horizon, as shown
here, this dark-to-light effect isn't a rigid rule.*

## HORIZON

The horizon is where the earth meets the sky. The horizon may be a line of distant mountains, the water's edge, or any combination of elements. Be sensitive to where you put the horizon line. The general principle is to place it in the upper or lower third of the landscape rather than right across the middle. Use the paper frame to position the horizon up or down in the composition until your eye tells you where it best belongs. But one thing is certain: water is flat. We've all seen photos taken in a boat with a tippy horizon. It's disconcerting. Our eye is accustomed to seeing a level water horizon and any pitched angle feels out of place. If you add a lake in the middle of the hills or a distant ocean, keep the water horizon flat and parallel to the top and bottom edges of the frame. Usually when I add a water element to a landscape I add fusible web to the wrong side first, and then cut it with a rotary cutter and a ruler to make sure

the edge is absolutely straight. For hand appliqué, I iron the seam allowance under to make sure it will remain straight when I stitch it in place.

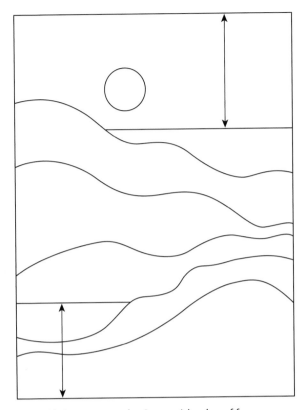

Lining up water horizons with edge of frame

## GETTING STARTED WITH A FREE-FORM LANDSCAPE

One way to begin is by drawing out a landscape on paper and following my methods for making a template pattern. Another method is to draw the landform cutting line directly on the fabric with pencil. Or you could just strike out, scissors in hand, and let the fabric inspire and lead your design. That's what I prefer to do, and I hope you try it and see what great fun it is. But if you prefer a more structured, planned approach, start by choosing one of the landscape projects and omit the steps involving the template pattern and fabric marking. Simply cut out the pieces freehand. Here are some guidelines for using the "Basic Landscape" pattern for the cut-and-collage process. Turn to page 15 for the pattern and instructions, and follow along with these steps.

1. Follow the pattern instructions to cut a muslin base and two 2"-wide L shapes for the frame.

2. Follow the number sequence in the pattern starting with the sky. Choose sky fabric and cut it out big enough to cover the muslin base. I always cut the sky and landform pieces a little larger to allow flexibility as the composition develops. Next prepare the water by adding fusible web to a piece of fabric a bit larger than the pattern states; 2" x 5" is a good size to use.

3. Cut all the pieces in the same number sequence as the pattern, but let your scissors be your pencil. Eyeing the pattern as a guide, cut each piece free form. Your scissors and your eye work together to evaluate each shape. Cut each landform shape without adding a seam allowance. In the photograph at top right, you'll see that I cut out fabrics in the same sequence as in the pattern, but with slight changes. Shape 3 no longer runs right across the landscape and I cut shape 5 to overlap the water. I also added an extra landform between 5 and 6. I felt the dark red landform of piece 6 needed a lighter, rusty highlight fabric behind it. This highlighting technique is a neat way to add narrow highlights of a "zinger" color to a landscape to liven up a color scheme, or to bring light into it if the colors are too dark. I described this technique in "Shadowland" (page 54). Evaluate your own landscape and decide which landform shape you'd like to highlight. Remove the chosen shape and lay it on top of two or three contrasting fabric strips. Cut all the layers as a single unit, following the outline of the top landform shape. Then slide them slightly apart—about 1/8"—to show thin lines of color. Because a single shape is repeated several times, this creates visual rhythm and adds strength to the design.

4. Now take the paper frame and start moving it around on the landscape. In the center photo, I moved the frame to make the landscape more horizontal. In the bottom photo, the frame is narrow and vertical. In the vertical landscape, I added a headland behind the water to add a greater sense of depth. Move the frame around the landscape to define different areas, and you'll discover that it can change the focus quite dramatically.

5. Play with the positioning of each piece; do you want to cut a few more valleys or change an angle? Perhaps you'd like to add additional hill shapes and introduce different colors. Cut it out to see what it looks like in the composition, and keep changing the composition until it pleases you. Remember to use the paper frame to evaluate each change. Be adventurous. Make it your own. But remember to keep the window closed so a breeze doesn't blow your loose pieces around while you're composing!

6. When you are happy with the landscape, pin it and stitch the pieces in place. Measure the opening of the frame size you have settled on. Trim away the outer edges of the landscape with a rotary cutter, leaving at least a ½" margin all the way around so it can be mounted into a mat frame. It's now ready for a fabric border or a mat frame.

At this point, you are well on the way to making your own unique landscapes. The more you make, the more the designs will flow.

Beach Glow *by Jo Diggs, 12¼" x 6¼"*

Jo used Mickey Lawler's hand-painted Skydyes fabrics as her inspiration in this captivating seascape study of light and reflections. Each fabric is carefully chosen to express the maximum quality of light. The blue water plays against a golden glow in the sky, with the warm sky tones being picked up in the cloud layers. Jo played around with this landscape off and on for a year before the perfect pieces of fabric completed it.

Ice Prisms *by Nancy Bergman, 28" x 25"*

Be a Tree! *by Reta Budd, 25½" x 35"*

Nancy lives in a pristine Canadian boreal forest region called Lake of the Woods, in northwestern Ontario, which has 14,000 islands. In that environment, Nancy studies the surrounding beauty and her quilts reflect its essence.

This quilt was inspired by photographs taken of the changing icescape on the lake in front of her house. The breakup of lake ice is the last act of winter and the prelude to spring. The forces of sun, wind, and rain etch the ice with patterns and it changes from chunky white floes to glistening ice, from black ice and open water to sparkling prisms.

Starting with a line drawing, Nancy paper pieced the design using her method for curved paper piecing. Cottons and reflective lamé convey the cold brittleness of the ice. The pine trees were thread painted on tulle and Solvy stabilizer, and then sewn onto the landscape. Beads and couched yarns are stitched in the foreground. The piece is machine quilted using metallic thread.

This lyrical landscape quilt is a portrait of a special tree that grows near Reta's farm in southern Ontario. It's machine appliquéd with some turned edges and some raw, and there's also hand and machine embroidery and hand quilting. Reta used fabric crayons to shade some areas, with threads and yarns hand couched for texture. Where the shade of the tree falls across the road, pieces of fabric are arranged vertically to keep the direction of the road true, and these are held in place with net and embroidery.

Reta describes her landscape as a "soulscape": "This tree has stood for more than 100 years as a symbol of strength, courage, hope. Now, the storms of life and the ravages of man have left their marks, but she still stands tall and straight and proud as if an unseen power sustains her. This quilt hangs in my mother's room in the nursing home where it gives her support and courage to face the days of her life."

*Pond with Reflections by Jo Diggs, 6" x 9"*

*Safe as Houses by Valerie Hearder, 30" x 41"*

Jo always displays a masterful use of fabric that captures the effects of light, even when working with opaque appliqué shapes. She constantly searches for fabrics to express light, especially fabrics that fade from light to dark and imply a light source. Jo says her fabrics end up looking like Swiss cheese because she cherry-picks the best area of the fabric, and jokes that her fabrics look like they are the result of the huge moths they have in Maine. Jo finds commercial fabrics an inspiration. This piece is mounted in a mat frame and, like all Jo's work, is hand appliquéd.

I made this quilt when we lived in Newfoundland—a rugged and dramatically beautiful island in the North Atlantic. The cold, misty weather was at first a challenge, but I soon fell in love with the landscape. This piece started with a tiny landscape in the center of the house-shaped quilt. I used some Skydyes hand-painted fabric and the others are commercial prints. Machine piecing, fusible appliqué, and machine quilting brought them all together.

As Seen with a Listening Heart *by Karen Colbourne Martin, 32½" x 21"*

Tide's Out *by Karen Colbourne Martin, 6½" x 4½"*

Karen's landscapes spring from her deep-rooted connection to Newfoundland, where her family has lived for generations. Karen uses her father's slides of old coastal fishing villages—many of which no longer exist because they were relocated to bigger centers—as a basis to make large-scale drawings. Freezer-paper templates are drawn and each piece is meticulously appliquéd and stitched in place. Karen uses mainly commercial fabrics. Her attention to detail is remarkable as she builds a house plank by fabric plank, or stitches in each fence pole. She exhibits a sensitive rendering of these places that are clearly so loved.

Blue Boats at Blue Rocks *by Laurie Swim, 32" x 19"*

Laurie lives in the charming ocean-side village of Blue Rocks, Nova Scotia, and this glowing piece is part of the series "The Ragged Shore." Look at how she captures the ever-changing light, reflections off the water, and contrasts and rich textures in the surrounding landscape. Laurie starts with photographic images and develops the composition from drawings to help acquaint herself with the shapes and the depth of field. The drawings form the templates for making the pattern. Laurie builds an impressionistic collage of the landscape through layering, machine quilting, and embroidery. She chooses diverse fabrics from many sources for their visual effect: dupioni silks, rayon, jacquard woven patterns, cottons and, for the sky, hand-painted iron-on transfer on poly-satin. The piece is not bound, but rather sewn to a cloth mat of silk.

East Coast Trails *by Margaret Vant Erve, 6" x 10"*

Newfoundland is renowned for its spectacular coastline and many hiking trails traversing the sea cliffs. I have walked the trail that Margaret portrays here. To create this piece, Margaret stretched habotai silk tightly in a frame and started painting with Pebeo water-based silk paints and gutta resist. Gutta forms a thin line to contain the paints within confined areas. Gutta was drawn across the horizon to separate the sky from the water. Margaret works wet on wet to achieve smooth results as she carefully paints each section and heat sets it before the gutta lines are washed out. This process is repeated around the clouds to enable her to paint within them. Pebeo transparent textile paints, which are less fluid, were used as a base color beneath the cliffs and plateau. Margaret then stretched the painting taut in an embroidery hoop and completed the trees and shrubs in free-motion machine stitching. She stretched the fabric again in the frame to stitch the rocky shoreline, which was entirely hand embroidered using long and short technique. Finally, the surf of the ocean was done in horizontal stitching using fine flat silks.

# RESOURCES

Most of these Web sites list retail outlets for their products.

## Heat Set Inks
Ranger Inks
www.rangerink.com

## Mickey Lawler Hand-Painted Sky Fabrics
www.skydyes.com

## Misty-Fuse Fusible Web
www.esteritaaustin.com/shoponline.htm

## Oil Paint Sticks
www.cedarcanyontextiles.com
Cedar Canyon carries Shiva Paintstiks; various brands are available from art-supply stores.

## South African Sun Print Fabrics
Langa Lapu Fabrics
www.langalapu.co.za

## Teflon Pressing Sheets and More
Many supplies used in this book can be found on Valerie's Web site, www.valeriehearder.com.

## Vanishing Muslin and Stabilizers
Sulky of America
www.sulky.com

# ABOUT THE AUTHOR

Valerie Hearder began making quilts in 1973. Her first small, framed landscapes were made in 1981, and soon afterward Valerie began teaching and, eventually, writing about them. Her quilting career has spanned 30 years and she has developed a reputation in the quilt world for positive and inspiring workshops. Her workshops have taken her to Europe, Japan, South Africa, the United Kingdom, Ireland, and throughout North America. Valerie's quilts have been exhibited internationally and have appeared in scores of publications. She has been awarded several honors, including the prestigious Dorothy McMurdie Award, presented by the Canadian Quilters Association for significant contribution to Canadian quilting. She was also included in 30 Distinguished Quilt Artists of the World, a juried exhibition in the Tokyo Dome. This is her second book on fabric landscapes. Valerie enjoys an idyllic country life in Nova Scotia, Canada, where she lives with her husband.

*Photo by Richard J. Hebb*